D1245410

PENNY PINCHING TIPS FOR THE MORALLY BANKRUPT

Libby Marshall

Atomic Vortex Press

ISBN-13: 978-1-7363969-1-9

Library of Congress Control Number: 2020925822
Printed in the United States of America

For my mom

CONTENTS

Penny Pinching Tips For The Morally Bankrupt

Caught in the rain? There's always a bucket of free umbrellas by the entrances of office buildings, restaurants, and homeless shelters.

Bring your own shopping bags to the grocery store to avoid a seven-cent plastic bag tax. That gives the government fewer funds to investigate your tax evasion.

Get a library card to check out books for free. Read how to smuggle elephant ivory on the black market.

Staples, paper, and pens aren't the only supplies you can get from the office. Kidnap a secretary. Lock her in your basement to run your home business wooing lonely housewives online to send money to your alias, Buff McCracken.

Ask for a friend's Netflix password. People usually use one password for everything so you can drain their bank accounts while binging the latest season of *Great British Bake Off*.

Knowledge is power when negotiating for a new home. Stakeout the house to learn the family's daily schedule. Send threatening letters, mentioning their children by name. They'll soon accept any offer. (For advanced penny pinchers, tell them if they remove their KitchenAid appliances, you'll kill their kitten.)

Volunteering is a free way to feel good about yourself. Start training seeing-eye dogs. Befriend members of the blind community. When they invite you over to their homes, steal their family heirlooms.

Having a child might seem like a large expense, but it is the only way to acquire a clean social security number. Name him Buff McCracken Jr.

Don't spend money on expensive gifts when you can make a personalized card for free. Force the secretary you kidnapped to make the cards based on the conversations with your family and friends she overheard through your vents.

Instead of turning on the air conditioner in the summer, open a bedroom window. Share this tip with your neighbors and you can cancel your porn subscription.

At your local ice cream parlor, get a free sweet treat by demanding to sample every flavor. The customers in line behind you will be so irate they won't notice they're being pickpocketed by Buff McCracken Jr.

Invest in organizations that are also morally bankrupt, such as Monsanto, Nestlé, and ISIS.

Always be willing to ask for a discount when making a purchase. If the cashier says no, bite your tongue so hard you spray blood everywhere. Scream that you need the discount because of the high cost of your syphilis medication. They won't be able to get the merchandise out of their store fast enough.

Skip your morning Starbucks and instead get free coffee at AA meetings. This is also a great place to meet people desperate for a charismatic leader to tell them how to live.

Need a new suit? Check obituaries for recently deceased men in your size. Bribe the funeral director with elephant ivory. While wearing your new suit, break into the homes of the dead man's loved ones. Wail and moan that the only way your soul can rest is if they leave hundred-dollar bills on your grave.

Instead of an expensive gym membership, get a free workout by promising a man one hundred dollars if he chases you through the forest. Once you're far enough out there, turn around, beat him senseless with an antique candlestick you stole from a blind person, and take his wallet.

Use the money you've made to take Buff McCracken Jr.

and the secretary who has succumbed to Stockholm Syndrome and is now your wife, on a tropical getaway to the Maldives. With beautiful beaches, high levels of corruption, and no extradition treaty to the US, it's the perfect place to spend the rest of your days on the beach sipping Kuramathi cocktails served by lovely local women.

Tip 10%.

Welcome To Our Tropical Resort Where No Guests Have Ever Been Torn Apart By Monkeys

Welcome to the Blue Bay Resort, Mr. and Mrs. Alvarez. I'm Stefan, the general manager and master of making sure this is a honeymoon you'll never forget. Rodrigo will take your bags and I'll show you around the property. For the past six years, Blue Bay Resort has been the pinnacle of Caribbean luxury. From white sand beaches to snorkeling adventures to delectable fresh seafood, every moment of your stay will be a moment in paradise.

And none of our guests have ever been torn apart by monkeys.

Because you've purchased our Premium package, you get these orange VIP wristbands. They give you front row seats for our nightly fire dance show. They also ensure that we know you are totally 100% human and not large hairless monkeys who have stolen the clothing of their victims in order to infiltrate the resort.

To your left is our Tranquility Pool. Yes Mr. Alvarez, the gate to the pool is four layers of triple reinforced carbon steel, but it's a standard safety measure. Sure, there's a barbed wire dome over the water, but it's for decorative purposes. Brutalist chic. And yes, that lifeguard is carrying a Remington MK 13 sniper rifle. Don't be concerned. It's just for show. If anything gets past the electric fence, there's really no stopping it.

I'm sorry to say we won't be offering our sunrise yoga or wind-surfing lessons. We are a bit short-staffed at the moment. But I assure you, all former employees are very much alive with all of their limbs and teeth. This shrine with photos of former guests and employees surrounded by flowers and incense is to commemorate just how alive and not flayed by monkeys that have learned to use knives they are.

Now we're passing our infirmary. Dr. Belmont is always on call, but we have so few injuries he might as well be on vacation! No, Mrs. Alvarez, I assure you a blood-soaked Dr. Belmont did not just run past us screaming, "I can't do this anymore. I can't lose another patient to those damn monkeys." Must have been a hallucination from jet lag.

Here's our stunning private beach. Please ignore the metal cages situated every ten feet along the beach, baited with tasty figs. They may look delicious, but touching the figs will trigger a three-foot long steel impalement spike. You should also ignore any monkeys impaled on the spikes. Even if the monkeys are pleading in rudimentary English, do not approach them. No Mr. Alvarez, the monkeys aren't dangerous, they're just having so much fun being impaled, we wouldn't want to ruin it by helping them.

Let me show you your Honeymoon Suite. There's a heart-shaped waterbed, a complimentary basket of massage oils, and a bottle of champagne in the mini-fridge. Go on, Mrs. Alvarez, open it up. That's a 2008... human arm. Um, must be from the previous guests. I'll have a word with the housekeeper. Her son was recently torn apart by monkeys, but that's no excuse.

What's that earsplitting siren? It's a normal Monkey Alarm. Rodrigo will put on his full-body Kevlar Monkey Suit, grab his electric Monkey Gun, and take care of it. Now, from this angle it looks as if a swarm of dozens of shrieking monkeys have overwhelmed Rodrigo and are ripping him limb from limb. But that's a trick of the light. Look this way and you'll see complimentary Mai Tais.

No, Mr. Alvarez, this is certainly not a Jurassic Park type situation where the hubris of man is being destroyed by the might of mother nature. I've never even heard of Dr. Knox Fritz, an esteemed primatologist who suffered a mental break after being struck by lightning eleven times. Why would a man even alter the genetics of Vervet Monkeys to give them giant muscular arms, humanlike intelligence, and teeth that are all fangs?

Mr. and Mrs. Alvarez, there's no need to take the last two seats on the helicopter escaping the island. Blue Bay Resort is perfectly safe. I've worked here for over three days and nothing bad has happened to me. What happened to the manager before me? He died in a monkey attack, but I don't see how that's relevant.

Okay, I'm going to stand here enjoying this magnificent white sand beach and sipping a Mai Tai while watching your helicopter become a speck on the horizon.

Ooh, figs!

Witnesses Of Historic Moments Who Missed The Point

The Resurrection of Jesus

So we opened the tomb and saw it was empty and I was like shit, a coyote must have gotten in there with the body. Everyone else was all, "it's a miracle." Meanwhile, I'm searching for this man-eating coyote. What if I got it and chained it up in my yard? I bet people would pay some silver to pet it or get its hair in a locket or something. A coyote that can eat a whole man in three days, bones and all? That's what I call a miracle. Anyway, I'm fired from tomb guarding duty.

The First Thanksgiving

Last week we had this huge harvest feast with the natives. I decided my contribution would be to make decorations. I scattered the table with leaves and made miniature versions of everyone out of sticks and mud. We were all sitting down to eat when John asks, "Mary, did you bring the clams?" And I say, "No, I was in charge of decorations." And then John holds up this piece of bark and it has my name next to clams and I say, "That must have been the other Mary who died of exposure." And he says, "No, that's your handwriting." And we're doing this in front of the guests and it's so uncomfortable. And John says really loud, "I guess we'll just have to try to enjoy this meal without clams. Dig in, I guess." And no one else thinks it's a big deal. There's lobster and crab, so who even misses clams? But whatever, it's not like anyone's going to remember this in a hundred years.

The Domestication of Rice

Ro asked me to come over and see his invention. He's got rice to grow where he wants it. It's in this big blob he's calling a paddy. I suggested that next time he should plant it in a shape.

For example, I could stand on the big hill and look at the paddy and see a flower or a star or a smiling face. Wouldn't that be fun? And Ro gets this dark look in his eye, then tries to beat me to death with a rock. To get him to stop, I say the blob is good. But really, I'm thinking about how some ideas are just ahead of their time.

The Sinking of The Titanic

Ok, since people have been asking, yes, I survived the sinking of the Titanic. But, that voyage was a disaster even before it sank! Greatest ship on earth, my sweet ass. They had a squash court, a gymnasium, and a library, but no billiards table. Not one on the entire ship. The only reason I bought a ticket was to practice billiards during the voyage, so when I got to America I could become a crack n' craw dilly of a pool shark. I got my complaint to the captain, who said billiards doesn't work on the ocean because of the waves. In the middle of our conversation, the ship hit the iceberg, so I didn't even get to challenge him to a game of pool once we got to America.

The Invention of The Printing Press

Everyone's been going crazy for my new printing press. Johannes, you're spreading literacy! Johannes, political thought can travel through the masses! Johannes, blah blah blah! I made this stupid thing to give myself sick-ass temporary tattoos. Everyone's like, ooh, let's put paper in and make "books." And I'm like, put your arm in there and I can put your mom's name and a heart made of barbed wire. I suggested that me and my friends get "The Gutenboys" on our chests, but none of them "got" it. Mostly because they can't read.

The Signing of The Magna Carta

All of us Barons are about to sign this royal charter of rights to limit the power of the King and I'm like, hey, just a quick addition. And the Archbishop is miffed, but he lets me say my piece. So I'm like, we've covered illegal imprisonment and feudal payments to the crown, but what about Serf Day?

Maybe we could outlaw that? And all the other Barons are really confused. I'm like, Serf Day, you know, the one day of the year when your serfs are in charge so they strip you naked and make you pull them around in a cart while they pelt you with rotten peaches? Then the most handsome serf gets to have sex with your wife, while you watch, trapped in a suit of armor? Serf Day? Every June 14th? And apparently, no one else has even heard of this holiday. So I laughed it off like I was making a joke and we all signed the Magna Carta. But when I get home I'm going to have a serious conversation with my serfs. And my wife.

Action Hero

"Karlakov has the nuclear codes tattooed on his heart. The only way to stop him from wiping out New York City is to find Karlakov, rip out his heart, and type in the code on the bomb strapped to The Statue of Liberty," screamed a woman in a lab coat as she hung on for dear life on the back of Jax Axel's souped-up hog-machine.

"Do you want to keep watching this?" I asked Nikki. It was a dumb action movie on TBS with exploding cars, sexy babes, and a badass hero who played by his own rules. The plot was tenuous and made harder to follow by the frequent commercial breaks for reverse mortgages and Life Alert.

Nikki had invited me to spend Sunday afternoon watching a movie in her dorm while her roommate did her triathlon practice, but neither of us was paying much attention. I was preoccupied with the chore wheel I had created for my dorm suite that only I cared about. Nikki was worried about the looming separation from her boyfriend who had gotten into medical school at Tulane.

"It's dumb to transfer closer, right?" she asked over the sound of Jax Axel strapping bombs to a Lamborghini.

I shrugged. Nikki would do what she wanted, and I didn't want to get caught on the wrong side of history. But yes, it was dumb.

"Come on Allen, I know you have an opinion." She shoved me gently, trying to shake a stance out of me. We'd been friends for two years, ever since getting cast on our campus's improv team, The Holy Goats.

"There are pros and cons to both," I said, then unable to help myself, "But I think that you, as a woman of color in STEM, will regret it if you interrupt your education for a guy." Shit.

Maybe if I hadn't chosen a Women's Studies minor, I would have been to keep my mouth shut. But here came Allen Campos, feminist ally.

Nikki pretended to watch the action movie, mulling over my words. Jax Axel pounded whiskey shots, preparing to confront Karlakov who was also his long-lost twin brother who he believed died in a truck explosion. The scantily clad bartender poured Jax Axel another shot, they had network TV appropriate sex in the back room of the bar, and he slipped her his phone number written on a napkin. She put it into her lacy black bra and winked. Nikki grabbed the remote and rewound, pausing on the napkin.

"Let's call it." She pulled out her phone and dialed.

"You know phone numbers in movies are fake, right? The 555 area code doesn't exist."

"It's ringing," said Nikki, putting the phone on speaker between us.

"Hello," said a gruff voice.

Nikki and I silently shrieked, arms flapping like headless chickens. "You say something, no you," we mouthed back and forth.

"How did you get this number?" demanded the voice. We heard a loud bang and the revving of an engine in the call's background. "I'm kind of in the middle of outrunning the Yugoslavian mob, so if you could call back later..."

"I'm the bartender. With the bra for a shirt," Nikki blurted.

"Oh, hello again," the voice growled, "After what we did on top of those beer crates, I bet you're ready for round two."

"Sure thing, big boy," said Nikki.

"What are you doing?" I whisper-demanded. Why was she playing along with this weirdo? This was some creep who had the phone number from the movie, waited for it to play on cable, and perved on anyone who called.

"It's him," Nikki pointed to the paused TV, "Jax Axel, from the movie." She un-paused it and fast-forwarded it to live. Jax

Axel was driving a stolen police car, talking on the phone, Yugo-slavian mobsters on his tail.

"You are not talking to a movie," I said, "This is obviously a freak who syncs up with the movie on TBS and…"

"Is someone there with you?" demanded Jax Axel, the same voice coming out of both the phone and the TV.

Nikki waved her arm, prompting me to talk. "I'm Allen… her friend."

"Hopefully you're gay because otherwise, I'll have to come back there and beat your ass." Jax Axel screeched to a halt and jumped out of the car and ran down a crowded pier.

"I'm bisexual, but-"

"Then I'll just have to beat up half of you." Jax Axel jumped over a cotton candy vendor, tufts of pink sugar attach-ing to the spikes on his leather jacket like silk from a flamboyant spider.

"Listen, Jax, I have a question for you," said Nikki. Bul-lets shattered mirrors as Jax Axel hid in the boardwalk fun-house. "My… friend's boyfriend got into medical school and she's wondering if she should follow him across the country."

Nikki was asking advice from a shared hallucination? Who knew the last time they had checked these old dorms for carbon monoxide?

Jax Axel strangled a clown holding a machine gun. "I know if I could spend one more day holding my Natalia's perfect ass, I would take it. But she died in a tragic plane explosion over the Adriatic Sea. One day I'll avenge her death, but until then I'm a mercenary for anyone with the long green."

"But Jax, they've only been dating for five months," I said, "and the friend is excelling in her computer science program. Anywhere else would be a downgrade for her future." I felt in-sane, trying to argue my case to a muscled action hero with tri-bal tattoos who was constantly sweating.

"After three months, Natalia and I were on our honey-moon on The Amalfi Coast. If only she hadn't gotten on that plane to Athens." Jax Axel did a swan dive off the pier, landing in a speed boat piloted by his best friend Maximus. "Weigh in here Max." Jax Axel explained the situation to his even more heavily tattooed compatriot.

"All I know," said Maximus as he piloted the speed boat toward The Statue of Liberty, "is I'd give anything to spend one more minute holding my sweet Andrea's beautiful breasts. If only she hadn't died in that motorcycle explosion."

"Listen," said Jax Axel, "before my old man died in a truck explosion, he always told me to follow my dreams. What is your friend's dream, sexy bartender? What does she want?"

The voice from the phone cut off as the movie paused for a commercial for Applebee's. Nikki hung up. We watched heaps of food swirl around the screen as Robert Palmer sang about Applebee's $7.99 Irresist-A-Bowls.

"I'm gonna stay," said Nikki, "Bill and I can do long-distance for a year. In those New York Times Vows pieces I read, every couple has an obstacle. This is ours."

I exhaled, both relieved for Nikki's future and glad I wasn't losing my best friend. "Now that you're staying, would you want to live together next year? I've gotta get out of the dorms. I found a turd in the shower last week."

"Hmm, I'm not sure." The movie resumed, Jax Axel scaling The Statue of Liberty as Maximus bled out in the water. "But I know who we can ask."

Millennial Gravestones

Here lies Esteban Block
He went viral in his little sister's TikTok

RIP Mercedes Dunn
She thought brunch lasted until three,
But they only served 'til one

Dearly departed Aiden Stix
Should have gone to the doctor
But lost his parent's insurance at twenty-six

Here lies Casey Sykes
Spent three hours editing a thirst trap
And only got fifteen likes

Audrey died driving her dad's old Ford
But no need to cry a wailing chorus
Her horoscope said
Never trust a Taurus

We will miss Moshe Gehring
They wanted an open-concept
Turns out that wall was load-bearing

Here lies Leslie Ossails
Her mother left her three voicemails

RIP Devonte Smett
The first man literally crushed by debt

Goodbye Theo Ansel
They made plans for Friday night
But forgot to cancel

Here lie Noura and Elliot Bischel
Married forty years
But never made it official

Signs

The sign said HORNY.

Sonya lay back in bed and sighed. She opened her bedside table, fishing around until she felt the smooth silicone of her vibrator. Pulling down her flannel pajama pants, she touched the kidney-shaped apparatus to her clitoris. Her fingers roved for the raised plus sign, and pressed, expecting the familiar buzz of pleasure. Instead, nothing.

The sign said FRUSTRATED.

She jammed the vibrator back in her drawer and closed her eyes. A few minutes of calm would cure frustrated. Sonya was lying in a meadow. A gentle breeze teased her dark curls. Butterflies felt safe to land on her arms. And what was this? A picnic basket full of fried catfish fillets and strawberry soda carried by actor Timothy Olyphant? Sonya peeked at the rectangular sign hanging on her bedroom wall.

The sign said HUNGRY.

A feeling Sonya could easily solve. She slipped down the hallway, trying not to wake her kids. If she could heat a blueberry muffin for twenty seconds in the microwave and enjoy it in solitude, the sign might just read nirvana.

"Mom!" shrieked Henry, "Talia is touching my dinosaurs even though you said they were mine and she should not touch them unless I said it was okay for her to touch them and I did not say that."

The sign said ANGRY.

"Talia, don't touch your brother's dinosaurs," yelled

Sonya. Damn it, all this yelling was going to wake up her husband.

Viktor emerged from the guest room pulling on a wrinkled Red Sox t-shirt. "What's the commotion?" He glanced at his overpriced smart watch, "at seven am on a Sunday?"

The sign said HATE.

"Dad!" said Henry as he wrapped himself around his father's leg, "Talia touched my dinosaurs even though I did not-"

"Hey bud," said Viktor, ruffling his spitting-image's hair, "I know what'll make this better. Why doesn't mommy whip us up some chocolate chip pancakes?"

"Can we have fresh squeezed orange juice?" asked Talia as she hurtled down the stairs. It was eerie how both kids so closely resembled their father. White-blonde curls, green eyes, and voices with steady growls, like crunching gravel on a driveway. Sonya wondered if her eggs had been empty, Viktor's sperm allowed to fill them up entirely.

"Fresh squeezed and pancakes? What do we think, Mama?" Viktor looked at Sonya, whose face was a carefully trained mirror. It reflected the expression he gave her, altering it enough that he didn't recognize it as his own.

"Sure we can, love bugs," said Sonya, "Go watch cartoons and I'll tell you when breakfast is ready."

"NO, I wanna help." Henry marched like a duck on stilts toward the kitchen with Talia running after him, screeching that she got to wear the purple apron.

Viktor wrapped an arm around Sonya's waist and buried his face in her hair. He smelled like stale morning breath and almonds. "I miss you. Are you sure I still need to sleep in the guest room?"

She looked up at him, trying to mirror his longing. "Sorry cholovik, you know I can't sleep with your snoring." For the entire fourteen years they had been together, she had encouraged him to see a doctor for his snoring. A potent mix of machismo and a perpetually packed schedule prevented it. Now Sonya was grateful to have an excuse to take their California King to herself while Viktor slept in the guest room.

"Neither of us will get any sleep in six months, anyway, mya koroleva," He kissed her on the head and rubbed her stomach. "Times three."

The sign said DREAD.

Henry took three bites of the from-scratch pancakes Sonya had poured into the shape of Mickey Mouse heads, spilled his cup of orange juice on the carpet, and informed the entire kitchen that he needed to poop. Talia sat at the table reading a book with a half-boy, half-dragon on the cover, her fork missing her mouth most of the time, too engrossed in the story. But not so engrossed she didn't complain that the orange juice tasted like worms and demanded Sonya run her glass through a mesh sieve until it was satisfactorily de-pulped.

"I was thinking," said Viktor, draining his cup of coffee, "we could go on a family bike ride." Viktor loved to suggest wholesome family activities, with no idea how much work they took to assemble.

The sign said EXHAUSTED.

After the bike ride, there had been Wiffle Ball, homemade sugar cookies, and Talia's living room violin recital. Viktor kept asking if Sonya felt well enough to do all this physical activity with three growing babies in her uterus. Truthfully, she didn't. All day she was swallowing back vomit, getting dizzy every time she stood up or sat down, and trying not to cry. But if running around like a mad woman gave her blessed bloody underwear, it would be worth it.

The sign said UNCOMFORTABLE.

Sonya took a shower. She tried her best to solve the feeling on the sign. Taking care of the smaller ones, HUNGRY, TIRED,

HORNY, was enough to counterbalance the larger ones she was ignoring. Not that there were consequences. The sign simply showed her in bold red font what she was feeling, often more specifically than she could articulate herself.

As Sonya scrubbed the grease out of her hair, she cried. It was a habit that started around the time she found out she was pregnant with Talia. Easy to blame red eyes on harsh shampoo. The actions had become so intertwined she wasn't sure she could step into a shower without bursting into tears.

Sonya assumed most people hated their lives. Or more accurately, most women hated their lives. Or even more accurately, most mothers hated their lives. The raccoon-eyed zombies she met in mommy and me classes must have the same distaste for the circumstances they fucked their way into.

Before Talia was born, in that precious year of freedom between senior year of college and the plus sign on the pregnancy test, Sonya had worked as a secretary at an advertising agency. She had left the sign at home, able to feel her feelings rather than name them. Was it HUNGRY or BORED or ANGRY? Either way, a bag of pretzels and flirting with the tattooed graphic designer solved it.

Now that home was her work, she checked the sign reflexively. Her husband would complain about incompetent paralegals or the new pitcher for the Red Sox or socialists in Congress, and she'd excuse herself to her bedroom. LONELY, DISGUSTED, INSECURE, the sign would tell her. The emotion would settle over her like a shroud. Once named, the feeling felt a thousand times stronger. It must be easier for other women. Women who feel a churning in their gut can blame it on indigestion. They don't have a framed sign blaring red letters in their face, putting a name to the churn.

The sign said BORED.

Henry, Talia, and Viktor (Kindergarten, Fifth Grade, White Shoe Law Firm) were gone. Sonya Swiffered the hardwood floors, bopping to the top forty. She had moved the sign into the dining room so she could watch her feelings change. HUNGRY, IMPATIENT, ANNOYED, a flicker of HAPPY when she saw a hummingbird out the kitchen window, then back to BORED. She didn't worry about a neighbor seeing her sign. She was the only one who could see the words. To anyone else it was a two-by-three foot piece of white poster board in a cheap black frame.

When they had first gotten together, both Juniors at Tufts, him in Econ and her still waffling between Russian Literature and Philosophy, Viktor had asked about the blank sign hanging above her dorm room mini fridge. He had an apartment off-campus, but she'd wanted to go back to her room instead, not quite trusting the Ukrainian, Jewish, and pathologically polite blonde boy who had walked out of all her mother's dreams for her only daughter.

"What does it look like to you?" she asked, pointing to the sign while trying to remember if she was wearing underwear without period stains.

"It's blank. Just an empty canvas. Is it a Duchamp thing?" Viktor put an arm around her waist and reached up to cup her breast. "Is your roommate...?"

"She's visiting her parents in Jacksonville."

Sonya had never watched the sign while she had sex. Adolescent fumbling in backseats, basements, and dorm room bunk beds hadn't given her the opportunity. As she braced her hands against her particle board desk, Viktor clutching her hips from behind, she watched the words flip. ANTICIPATION, PLEASURE, SURPRISE, EMBARRASSMENT, ECSTASY.

Two months later, the sign said LOVE.

Fourteen years later, it did not.

The sign said HUNGRY.

As Sonya rifled through the fridge, looking for a wedge of Wednesday night's lasagna to reheat for lunch, the doorbell rang. She checked her outfit, Viktor's Harvard Law sweatshirt, yoga pants, and an old bra she'd ripped the under wire out of. Good enough for the UPS guy. But instead of a man bringing her a brown box of nonsense she'd impulse ordered from Amazon, she found her neighbor Dasha.

"Have I got news for you," Dasha said as she swept past Sonya. Dasha wore an all-black athleisure ensemble and perched herself on the arm of the couch, looking even more like an underfed crow than usual.

The sign said ANNOYED.

"A new family is moving into the Geiser place. The moving company called and asked if it was ok to block my driveway for the afternoon."

"What did you say?" Sonya sat on the couch, knowing that the quickest way to an empty home was allowing Dasha to spill her gossip. Dasha thought they were close friends just because they had kids in the same grade and their parents had grown up in countries annexed by the Soviet Union.

"I said sure. Once they're moved in, we should bring them a treat. A welcome to the neighborhood gift." And a chance to snoop up close rather than relying on the binoculars that Dasha swore were for birdwatching. "How about we make them a Medovik?"

"Are they Russian?"

"I don't know. But we need to keep our culture strong. I have Maxim enrolled in Romanian language classes online, and we're planning a trip to Moldova for spring break."

"Ok. A Medovik sounds good."

The sign said FRUSTRATED.

"Perfect. Let's plan on popping by tomorrow. You bring the Medovik and I'll find coupons to local businesses in my coupon drawer." Dasha stood up, kissed Sonya on both cheeks, and flitted out the door.

The sign said RAGE.

A new feeling for Sonya regarding Dasha. Usually when Dasha made her gossipy visits, the sign said ANNOYED, IRKED, BORED. But Dasha had volunteered Sonya to spend four hours assembling the thin layers of a finicky Russian honey cake. As if she had to energy to assemble a dessert for strangers, when she could barely throw together some orange slices and capri sun for her own son's soccer games. She saw a twelve pack of assorted Costco muffins sitting unopened on her counter.

The sign said PLEASED.

"Mom, what's onomatopoeia?" asked Talia. Sonya was whisking eggs to coat homemade chicken tenders. Talia sat at the counter, worksheets scattered around her.

"I don't know, Talia. What is it?" Talia never asked her mother questions she didn't already know the answer to. She'd ask Viktor how the moon changed shape or why tigers had stripes, satisfied with whatever answer he pulled out of his ass. But for Sonya, she reserved questions like the steps of the water cycle or the year Lincoln was assassinated. Sonya suspected it was the same impulse that drove boys to challenge their fathers to physical fights that fueled Talia's questions. Proving she was smarter than her dumb old housewife mom.

"It's the formation of a word from a sound associated with what is named," Talia recited, "Can you give me an example?"

"Crash, bang, pow," Sonya replied, crunching Ritz crackers to coat her chicken. Henry whipped through the kitchen holding a large dirty stick. "Henry, the outside doesn't come inside."

"I said AN example, not three examples." Talia resumed her homework, her intellectual superiority satisfied. Daddy's little prosecutor.

"I'm a wizard!" shrieked Henry. He waved the stick around him, knocking over the porcelain camel Viktor's mother had brought them from her trip to The Holy Land. It shattered into a dozen pieces.

"Dammit Henry," said Sonya. Sonya's chest constricted and ice pooled at the back of her head. What was this feeling? All she wanted to do was run into her bedroom and check the sign.

"Dammit Henry," shrieked Talia, "Dammit Henry, Dammit, Dammit, Dammit."

"Talia, language." Sonya rushed over to grab the stick from Henry. "Henry, what have we said about playing rough near breakables?"

Henry threw himself on the ground and kicked his tiny legs. "I'm sorry. I'm sorry. I'm sorry."

"What are you sorry for, moi dorogi?" said Viktor as he strode through the front door carrying two greasy McDonald's bags.

"Daddy brought dinner!" Both kids ran toward him for hugs and Happy Meals.

"I thought I'd give you a night off," he said, winking at Sonya.

"Thanks, babe." She poured the egg wash down the drain, put the chicken back in the fridge, and turned off the oven, which was keeping the baked beans and dinner rolls warm. Her scalp itched, and she felt grease on her skin. She needed a shower. Or she needed to cry.

"Daddy, Henry broke Grandma's special camel," said Talia. Henry burst into tears. Talia took this opportunity to snatch the plastic wrapped Happy Meal toy from his hands.

"It's ok, Henry." Viktor scooped up the weeping boy. "I'm sure Mommy can fix it. You and her could make it a fun project. How's that?"

Sonya's eyes burned, a tangle of iron thorns pressed on her ribs, and the world shrank to a pinpoint. She ran out of the kitchen, back to her bedroom, and locked the door.

The sign said ANGRY.

Seemed about right.

Viktor knocked on the bedroom door. "Hon, is it morning sickness? Do you need a cold cloth?"

LOATHE. ABHOR. DETEST. EXECRATE. The sign whizzed through every word for hate she knew and a few she didn't. COMMINATE. SCORN. ABOMINATE. MALEDICT.

"I'm fine. Just lightheaded," she yelled at the door.

"Lie down. I'll feed the kids. Love you."

Oh, how she regretted putting that OBGYN appointment on the family's shared Google Calendar. She could have terminated the pregnancy, no fuss, no muss. But when Viktor had seen the appointment with Dr. Shelman and surprised her at the office with a dozen roses, she couldn't ask for an abortion. Not with her husband in the room, jumping with joy at the positive pregnancy test, calling his mom with the good news.

And when the ultrasound tech had announced it was triplets, Viktor actually cried. Big snotty sniffs as he looked at the three fetal blobs on the grainy monitor. But to Sonya, the clusters of cells rapidly dividing in her uterus were sentencing her to three more concurrent life sentences. Eighteen years was such bullshit. These zygotes would be home every college break, asking for money for med school, having her babysit their spawn when they reproduced. Sonya agreed with people who said motherhood wasn't an actual job. Because an actual job you could quit.

For a moment she considered rejoining her family in the kitchen. Using the pregnancy as an excuse to house a double cheeseburger or two. But she resisted, knowing she wouldn't enjoy the meal unless she could eat it in peace. Reheated McDonald's alone was infinitely better than fresh McDonald's together.

An hour of scrolling Instagram in bed later, she heard the kids running up the stairs to watch TV in the playroom and Viktor shutting the door to his office. She slunk down the hallway to the kitchen. She put the beans and rolls from the oven into Tupperware to be used at a future dinner. An explosion of paper wrappers, ketchup packets, and half eaten chicken nuggets littered the counter. She grabbed handfuls of greasy paper and jammed it into the trash can, filling it to the brim.

She tied the red plastic strings together, hauled the heavy bag out of the can, and carried it through the garage out to the trash bins at the side of their house. As she lifted up the garbage bin lid, she noticed a gray blob near Henry's discarded tricycle. An opossum stood frozen in the motion light. Sonya froze too. Garbage juice dripped onto her bare foot. The opossum's needle teeth glistened, and it let out a slow hiss, like air being let out of an evil basketball.

"Hey, move it, asshole," yelled a man from the sidewalk.

"Who the fuck are you calling asshole? This is my fucking house." Sonya gripped the Hefty bag so hard her fingers tore into the plastic. What a relief for her anger to find a deserving target.

"Oh shit, sorry," said the man as he walked toward her. He was a handsome guy, forty give or take five years, wearing running gear. Tattoos of leaves covered his arms and legs. Near his feet the leaves were dry and brittle, moving into a red and gold explosion up his legs, and fresh green up his arms. Sonya imagined her fingers snaking up the trunk of his spine, tracing the veins of the leaves with her fingertips. She'd always had a thing for guys with tattoos. Perhaps a response to her mother's warnings about men with tattoos being drug addicted psychopaths.

The man picked up Henry's trike and nudged the opossum toward the yard. It hissed, then retreated under an azalea bush.

"I wasn't talking to you," he said, putting down the trike, "I was talking to that fucker. I'm a vegetarian, but I'd kill every opossum in America if you gave me the chance."

Sonya nodded. Without the sign she couldn't be sure of her feelings, but she'd bet every penny in her bank account the sign in her empty bedroom blared red with LUST. The man was also staring at Sonya, his eyes catching on the nipples visible through her thin gray t-shirt.

"How would you do it?" she asked.

"Do what?"

"Kill them all. The opossums."

"Oh, uh, I was thinking, if someone came to my house with a button and they said, press it and all the opossums die, I'd press it. No hesitation."

"You wouldn't want to do it yourself?"

"No, I wouldn't want to be the Johnny Appleseed of killing opossums. I don't care that much." He stepped toward her. Was anyone watching them? Nosy Dasha with her binoculars, or another jogger on the street, or Viktor from his office window. All three possibilities excited her.

What if she fucked him? His lithe body pressing her against the side of her house as she gripped onto the brick for dear life. Another man swirling his tongue on her nipple. Another man pressing his fingers inside her, making sure she was wet enough to enter. Another man fucking her, quickly, quickly, quickly, both of them knowing someone could catch them at any moment.

"You're dripping."

"What - I...?" She snapped out of her reverie.

"The garbage," he said, pointing to the bag she still held, "it's dripping on your feet."

"Oh." She opened the garbage bin lid and threw in the bag. Her neck was on fire and her stomach was filled with helium. God, how she wanted to run inside to make sure how she felt, but if she left, she might never see him again.

"Try the Glad ForceFlex. Since my wife started buying those we haven't-"

"Do you want to fuck?" Her hair was a rat's nest and her feet smelled like week old melon rind.

"Pardon?" He blinked and stared at her mouth. His eyes laser focused to not misunderstand her next words.

"I said, do you want to fuck? Me?"

"I'm married." He raised his left hand to show her the gold band.

She raised hers too. "I'm pregnant."

The man turned a full circle, as though a group of people were going to appear from behind a shrub and yell that this was a prank. The green leaves on his arms fluttered as he clenched and unclenched his fingers. She watched him harden through his thin running shorts.

"That's okay," she said, turning to go back into the house. "If you don't want to…"

In an instant he had her pinned against the brick wall, his mouth pressed against hers. She pushed down her leggings and pulled aside the crotch of her underwear. He pulled down his shorts, poised to enter her. She stroked his ribs, pulling up his shirt to reveal flowers bursting over his torso.

"You sure?" he panted into her ear.

"Yes. Consent. Yes."

Sonya lost herself in the sensations, in the forbidden thrill of fucking a man other than her husband for the first time in fourteen years. Her back on the brick wall, his hand gripping her thigh, their breath fogging together in the cool night air. GOOD, GOOD, GOOD was all she could summon to name her feelings, but it was enough.

The orgasm surprised her. Her body shuddering so suddenly it made her choke, coughing as she leaned into his sweaty neck. He kept going for another minute, pumping away at her oversensitive flesh, until he moaned, drooling on her t-shirt. He stepped back and pulled up his shorts. She yanked up her leggings. They stood there in the glow of the motion light. The chirps of cicadas, the howls of the neighbor's basset hounds, and the shrieks of kids playing in an above ground pool reminded Sonya she was not in an alternate dimension without consequences, but firmly here outside her family's house in Newton, Massachusetts with another man's semen dripping into her panties.

"That was great," he said, sticking out a leafy green hand, "Um, I'm Kane."

"Yeah, thanks," she said, shaking his hand. No way was she

letting this man know her name. He already knew where she lived. She imagined him knocking on their front door and telling Viktor what she'd done. He'd be disappointed, but she knew he wouldn't leave. Not with three babies on the way. He'd never let himself look like that type of monster. There would be counseling and trust building exercises and in depth talks about the why and the how of her betrayal. When there had been no more thought behind it than when she snuck an Almond Joy into her purse at the Wegmans.

"I gotta go," he said, "Five more miles, you know."

Before he could run off, she slipped back inside her house and ran to her bedroom. What would the sign say? HAPPY, GUILTY, EXCITED? When she entered her room, she found Talia splayed on her bed, reading a book featuring a fairy riding a unicorn on its cover. A tiny female Viktor smiling up at her from their marriage bed.

"Henry is being loud and Daddy's working, so I'm reading in here." She held up the book. "I can read it to you. Geminia Dewdrop, a fairy princess, is going into battle against Zephyrus Bitterthistle, the changeling king."

"Sure, honey." She took another step into the room to turn to look at her sign.

Sonya was half-listening as Talia asked her a question. She rolled her eyes. Another round of prove you're smarter than Mom.

"Sorry, honey?"

"What's the word lust mean?"

"Is that in your book?" What kind of language was being allowed in middle grade fantasy novels these days?

"No, it was on your painting earlier."

Fuck.

"What are you talking about? That's an old blank piece of art, Talia." Fuck fuck fuck fuck fuck.

"No, now it says fear. Is it a digital picture frame like Kami's mom has?"

Bless her precocious know-it-all spawn. "Exactly. It says

random words. It's art."

"Hmm," said Talia. "Because I've seen it before, and it didn't say anything."

"Um... ahh... well." Sonya had nothing. No satisfactory explanation. No one, not a roommate, a friend, a guest, had ever commented on the sign past asking her why she had a blank white canvas hanging on her wall. "Do you want ice cream?"

Talia eyed her mother, weighing the knowledge of what the sign was versus a bribery scoop of Ben & Jerry's Tonight Dough. "Does Henry get any?"

"No, just you." Sonya imagined Talia lording her extra dessert over Henry and the chaos that would ensue. "But you can't tell him you got ice cream. This is our secret. You're almost a woman. You need to learn how to keep secrets."

"Do you have any secrets?"

"Of course I do, every woman does."

The sign said HELPLESS.

"Are those muffins homemade, at least?" asked Dasha as they stood on the doorstep of the new neighbors.

"They're made by the fine people at Costco." Sonya's stomach hurt, her expanding belly pressing against the stiff denim of her high waisted jeans. In a fit of denial, she refused to dig in the basement for the boxes of her old maternity clothes. Putting on a leopard print muumuu was a white flag she wasn't ready to raise.

"We're not making a good impression. I thought you were making a Medovik?" Dasha glared at Sonya, refusing to ring the doorbell until Sonya felt a proper amount of shame.

"Sorry, Dasha. I was tired." Tired from tossing and turning all night at what Talia's ability to read her sign might mean. Then feeling guilty that she wasn't tossing and turning over cheating on her husband. She swallowed bile, her breakfast granola bar and orange juice revisiting her mouth.

"We're all tired, Sonya. That doesn't mean-"

"I'm pregnant with triplets." Playing three baby cards was a powerful hand.

"Congratulations! Here, you shouldn't be carrying those." Dasha took the wicker bowl of muffins from Sonya. "How far along? We must celebrate after this! Sparkling grape juice in my sunroom."

The leeches were good for something. She wondered if the sign said GRATITUDE. She'd hidden it at the top of her closet, stepping up on a hard suitcase every time she wanted to get it down and see how she was feeling. Sonya plastered on a smile and rang the doorbell.

A forty-something black woman with dreadlocks tied back with a bandana and wearing a faded Nike t-shirt opened the door. She looked confused until she saw the muffins in Dasha's hands.

"You must be the welcome wagon," she said, wiping her hands on her jeans. "I'm Mira."

"I'm Dasha and that's Sonya. Welcome to the cul-de-sac!" Without invitation, Dasha elbowed past the woman. Boxes lined the walls, furniture was still wrapped in plastic, and the living room smelled of fresh paint.

"Um, I have Coke in the fridge." Mira raised her eyebrows at the welcome wagon barging into her home.

"Diet if you've got it," said Dasha, taking herself on a tour. "There's so much nice hardwood. The last owners kept it covered up by those filthy rugs. And FYI they fostered a lot of old cats, so if you're doing any gardening, don't be surprised if you find a few shoeboxes out there, if you know what I mean."

Sonya sat on a plastic covered recliner in the living room. She turned her face up, trying to swallow the vomit. The ceiling was a half-finished kaleidoscope of colors. Blue, green, red, yellow, in triangles sectioned off by blue tape. Her head was numb, the vomit still rising, her body jerked forward as she sprayed blood and bile across the floor.

"Here's a Coke-" Mira screamed and dropped the cans. One exploded, fizzing across the floor. "Fuck, I'll call 911."

Sonya heard footsteps rushing down the stairs. Hands rubbed her back. SICK, SICK, SICK. But what was this other feeling? The tingle in her fingers. This thudding in her ears. RELIEF, FEAR, GUILT?

"A woman is vomiting blood," said Mira to the 911 operator. "She's my neighbor. Yeah, my address is-"

"She's pregnant." Sonya looked up and saw Kane leaning over her.

"She said it. Before you came in," he lied smoothly to his wife.

Kane wasn't wearing a shirt. Sonya saw the gorgeous flowers tattooed across his torso. Twisting vines of gardenias, peonies, and violets in colorful bursts and swirls. She leaned into his chest, pressing her face to a cluster of red roses so real she could smell their velvety aroma. Cocooned in his leafy limbs, her mind gave her what she needed. Floating in front of her, she saw the large red word, SAFE.

The doctor hadn't said bed rest. He'd said stress induced gastritis. Neutral foods. Prilosec. Plenty of fluids. Rest up. Call if it happens again. But somehow all those words added up to Viktor insisting she stay in bed for the rest of her pregnancy.

She'd tried to argue. "Six months of staring at the walls? Viktor, what about the kids? What about the house?" He was driving them home from the hospital, five miles per hour under the speed limit.

"We'll hire a nanny. A housekeeper. My mom can live with us. Your mom can live with us. Whatever. Do you want to lose these babies, Sonya?"

Yes. "No."

The sign said DESPERATE.

It was a fucked up monkey's paw of a situation. She'd wanted to be with her sign all the time and now here she was, confined to her bedroom all day and all night. Talia and Henry were forbidden to enter her room, so it had been safe to put her sign back on the wall. Now she never had to guess what she was feeling. It was always there. Even in sleep. Gone were dreams about high school hallways, or mountain ranges, or meeting handsome tattooed men in dive bars. Her mind could not leave behind the security of her sign, so all her dreams took place between the four eggshell white walls of her bedroom.

Viktor hired Gloriana the next day, with glowing recommendations from two wives of partners at the law firm. When Viktor introduced the middle-aged Brazilian woman, he'd apologized he couldn't find someone Ukrainian, but Sonya liked that her friendly warden couldn't understand when she muttered profanities under her breath.

Gloriana arrived at six am and left at eight pm. The hours had seemed preposterous at first. The kids were in school until three thirty, then in after-school activities (T-Ball and Violin and Math Rangers and Girl Scouts) until five or six. It didn't make any sense. Until she realized the nanny was for her.

Bringing her meals. Cleaning out her vomit trash can. Accompanying her on her daily journeys from the bed to the bathroom. Keeping her apprised of her children's comings and goings. Escorting her to doctor's appointments. After a few days, Sonya felt less like a person and more like a living terrarium, cleaned and cared for only to keep the creatures inside alive. The three genderless parasites making her gums bleed and her stomach roil.

Gloriana was kind, patient, and always had a sugar free Werther's caramel in her pocket. Sonya had no gripe with her. She was doing her job. And by the sounds of joy her kids made when Gloriana did anything from serving her famous baked mac and cheese to braiding Talia's hair to talking to Henry about dinosaurs, she was a more than suitable substitute for the bedbound harpy formerly known as Mom.

Was this her punishment? Use one unobserved moment to cheat on your husband and never have a moment to yourself again. The sign sometimes said GUILT, but it wasn't GUILT at the infidelity, but GUILT that she didn't feel GUILTIER. Perhaps it was because it had been so quick. She hadn't carried on a months-long affair, having afternoon trysts at seedy motels. That was cheating. What she did was a blip. A seven minute flight of fancy.

Viktor was a good man. Viktor is a good man. Viktor will be a good man. And what was the alternative? Leave while pregnant with triplets? Rent a crappy studio apartment and take care of three screaming infants on her own while seeing Talia and Henry every other week? No, the only way forward was through.

The sign said RESENTFUL.

When Talia and Henry arrived home every day from school, they stood in the doorway, updating her on such riveting topics as Brandan R. dipping his pizza in chocolate milk at lunch and Mrs. Wenders moving Talia up to the Purple reading group. Talia didn't mention the sign again, but Sonya saw her leaning forward in the doorway, trying to see it. A glint in Talia's greedy eyes reminded Sonya of her first interactions with the sign.

One day on her wall was a *Saved By The Bell* poster, the whole gang sitting on two red and blue ladders. The next day there hung a sign that said CONFUSED. Sonya stared at it and watched the letters fade and reform into HUNGRY. Her stomach growled. The lunch at Jewish Day Camp hadn't been particularly filling.

"Mom, mom, mom," Sonya screeched as she flew down the stairs, "There's a poster in my room that changes words."

She found her mom wiping the kitchen counter with a damp sponge. Sonya's mother was a quiet woman, never raising her voice except when she yelled for the family's poodle Laika to come in from the yard. She was a perpetual motion machine who had been known to get caught sleep-cleaning, pushing a dust mop as she shambled through their already spotless home.

"What's the matter, Kroshka?" asked her mother, scrubbing at a stain on the counter only she could see.

Sonya paused to assemble her sentences. "There's a poster in my room. A new one. It says words."

"Can you grab the beef from the freezer? I want to defrost it for dinner."

"No, you're not listening. Come see." Already taller than her diminutive mother, Sonya had no problem dragging her up the stairs to her bedroom.

"See, it says FRUSTRATED. Before it said HUNGRY. It's changing. It must be magic."

Her mother frowned at the poster. "I don't see it."

"What do you mean you don't see it?" She dragged her mother's hand to touch the poster. "It's right there. See! Now it says SHOCKED."

"It's a white plakat. Blank." Her mother took her hand back. "I don't have time for your imaginations, Sonya."

"But mama..."

"Ni, Sonya. Wash your hands. I need you to slice onions."

The sign said HUNGRY

"Dinner," said Gloriana as she set the four legged tray on the bed. "Baked chicken, corn, and green beans. And a glass of 2% milk. It's good for the babies' bones." As if the monsters needed to be any stronger, kicking and punching, treating her uterus as their own personal UFC octagon.

After two months of Gloriana's dinners, Sonya wondered if the woman knew any other method of chicken preparation besides baking it without salt. But of course she did. Viktor had raved about Gloriana's chicken tikka masala, even having her write down the recipe so Sonya could reproduce it when Gloriana was gone. The unseasoned meals were fulfilling an order from Viktor for only healthy food to be brought to the human incubator.

The sign said EXCITED.

"Ring the bell when you finish up," said Gloriana, "I can slice you up an apple with almond butter for dessert."

Through the open door they heard Talia yell, "There's a turtle on the driveway. Can we keep him?"

Gloriana patted Sonya on the head. "I'll take care of that. Enjoy your dinner." She shut the door, leaving Sonya to choke down her bland meal. Not even a pool of sauce to dip the chicken in. She'd give her left tit for a packet of honey mustard.

The sign said HAPPY.

Wrong. But the sign was never wrong. Ever since it had appeared in her bedroom at age twelve, the feeling had matched precisely with her interior. Even feelings that might not be so obvious (JEALOUS, INSECURE, REMORSEFUL), when she held them in her heart always ended up matching what she really felt. But HAPPY was not unsalted chicken. HAPPY was not spending all day watching every season of Grey's Anatomy for the fourth time. HAPPY was not being trapped inside while simultaneously having things trapped inside of you.

"But what if we cleaned him?" yelled Talia, "Then he wouldn't have the salmo-niella!"

Gloriana's calm reply was drowned out by Talia's whine. "But he *loves* me."

The sign said OUTRAGED.

Sonya rolled her eyes at Talia's stubbornness. That she got from Sonya. The proof that her daughter was at least partly hers.

Talia sobbed as she ran up the stairs.

The sign said SAD.

In the following weeks, Sonya lost her psychic tug of war. At first, most of the feelings were hers. RESENTFUL, BORED, TIRED. But a few wild GLEEFUL, AMUSED, SURPRISED, snuck in, the strongest feelings of Talia's school day slipping into Sonya's reality. Every time she saw a feeling that wasn't hers, Sonya hyperventilated, trying to work herself into a strong enough feeling to eclipse her daughter. The babies writhed, punching sensitive organs, and the sharp pain was enough to bring the sign back into her emotional orbit.

Sonya was clinging onto the sheer face of an icy cliff, any ground regained, lost at once as she grew weaker, slipping further down. Talia stood above her, hitting Sonya's grasping fingers with an ice pick, weakening her grip until the inevitable fall into the icy abyss.

It was worse when Talia was in the house. Sonya banned the children from entering her bedroom, saying their noise upset the babies, but it was really to keep Talia away from the sign. She was afraid that if Talia got too close, the sign would succumb to her gravity, and she'd lose it forever. But even with the ban in place, the sign went blank for hours at a time. Unsteady on her feet, she'd get up and beg with the sign, plead with it to tell her how she felt. Gloriana would hear her and guide her back into bed. Finally, the sign would say a word again and Sonya could relax.

Wild schemes raced through her head. They could send Talia to boarding school in Europe. It would be good for her to experience other cultures and perhaps an ocean would be enough distance to mitigate her strong feelings. During a particularly manic episode (the sign had been blank for five hours) Sonya considered Talia's death. Not in any concrete, bashing her daughter's head in with a shovel and burying her in the backyard way, but in the murky way anyone fantasizes about the death of a loved one. A tragic accident, a courageous battle with a terminal disease, saving a baby from a burning building. Then words would reappear, and the sign would blare GUILTY at her for even entertaining the thought of her eleven-year-old dying from smoke inhalation.

What Sonya needed was a time machine. A way to go back to that twenty-year-old girl in that crappy dorm room and warn her about her future. To take her to get an IUD and tell her that no matter how nice the tax break was or how much she wanted to wear a fluffy white ball gown, never to get married. And when she was back there, she'd rip up the sign. Without it, it would be easier to trust herself. To be on her own. To know what she wanted. After years of depending on the sign to tell her how she felt, it had been so easy to depend on Viktor for love, stability, reassurance. Perhaps if she'd been a bit more unmoored, she wouldn't have so willingly docked in the first harbor she entered.

The sign said

When Gloriana had taken her to her monthly check-up the sign had been fine, flipping through her feelings until Gloriana escorted her out to the car. But when she'd returned, after being poked and prodded and assured that all three leeches were big and strong and to keep doing whatever she's doing, the sign was blank. Sonya took a nap; sure the words would be there when she woke up.

The sign said

She heaved herself out of bed and stood in front of the sign, staring it down, begging the red words to form in front of her eyes. She thought she felt angry, but without the sign she couldn't be sure.

The sign said

After the first twenty-four hours of blankness the blinding panic dissipated. Sonya's heart had been dipped in Novocain; a throbbing numbness pumped through her veins.

The sign said

Viktor laid next to her in the evenings reading John Grisham on his Kindle getting pretzel crumbs on the duvet.

The sign said

Henry drew a picture of her and him holding hands outside of a blob that was their house with the title Bast Mom Evr.

The sign said

For an entire day she sat on the toilet doing nothing but shitting, vomiting, and choking down glugs of Gatorade.

The sign said

On day four, she stopped glancing at the sign, the Pavlovian response fading. On day five, she asked Gloriana for a pen and paper and tried writing her feelings for herself. They were all wrong, but with no guide for her to check her work, why couldn't that gurgle in her stomach be JOY? Why not feel HAPPY when she looked in the bathroom mirror and saw a tangle of stretch marks rising up her belly? She could LOVE it when Talia left a package of Oreos outside her door so the babies could have a treat.

By day ten, she was giddy with self-delusion. Terrible feelings were so much easier to ignore if they weren't blared at you in red ink. It had felt so futile, the inevitable slide into SAD. While there were some aspects of her life that could not be changed (five kids and a fifteen-year mortgage) there were so many things that could be improved. Now that she was not stuck to her home, afraid to be too far away from the sign, Sonya could join a book club or help at a food pantry or take up pottery. She could talk to Viktor when she was upset, rather than keeping it between her and her sign, no longer a silent third party in their marriage. And most importantly, she could keep Talia safe.

The sign said

"I'm going out to get groceries," said Gloriana from the doorway, "Anything special you want me to pick up?"

"Could you run by Sugar Sisters, the bakery by the Target?" asked Sonya, laying on a mound of body pillows reading a book about how French women raise their babies. "Please, pick up my order. It should be a tiramisu and cookies under our last name."

"Sure thing," said Gloriana. "A special occasion?"

"It's the anniversary of our first date, me and Viktor." Sonya blushed, again that awkward girl who thought Victoria's Secret body spray was the key to a man's heart.

"Aww," said Gloriana, "you two are so precious. That man really loves you."

Sonya smiled. Maybe she could love him too.

When Sonya heard Gloriana close the front door, she got up and took the sign off the wall. The thick poster board was no match for her knees as she folded it once, twice, three times, until it was a thick square. Holding onto the wall to support her newly front heavy frame, she stumbled down the hallway, out to the garage, and through the side door to the garbage bins.

No opossums or tattooed men met her in the afternoon sun. Just the smell of molding pizza rolls wafted from the trash as she jammed the sign inside. Sonya felt… COMPLETION? SAT-ISFACTION? ACCOMPLISHMENT? Why not all three? A bullet dodged, not for her, but for her daughter. No time machine could take Sonya back to her past, but she could still act in Talia's present.

That evening, Sonya asked Gloriana to help her with her plan. First Sonya showered. She still cried as she lathered with orange blossom suds. Not all habits were so easily broken. She put on a blue gingham maternity dress left over from her pregnancy with Henry. She'd faced the fact of her expanding body and asked Gloriana to dig her boxes of maternity clothes out from the basement. The three tiny gremlins kicked her in the liver as she coaxed her thick pregnancy hair into a romantic updo.

"Settle down, malenki monstri," she said, rubbing her belly. She hummed a lullaby as she struggled with bobby pins and the dervishes stopped whirling. Perhaps these three got more of her genes than Viktor's. She imagined a serious, dark haired girl. Sonya's own face in miniature. Raising three little lives without red words blaring at her, compounding the bad feelings that came from sleep deprivation and bleeding nipples. A chance to be, if not an outstanding mother, at least one not full of self-loathing.

Gloriana helped her out to the front porch and settled her in a wicker patio chair, with plenty of pillows for lumbar support. Viktor and the kids were kicking a soccer ball around the front yard.

"Talia, Henry," yelled Gloriana, "There are cookies in the kitchen for boys and girls who wash their hands with soap and water!"

The kids rushed past, then doubled back. Stunned to see their very pregnant mother, a goddess of fertility on the porch.

"Mommy!" Henry and Talia threw themselves at their mother, pressing their scalding bodies to her.

"Hey kids, let mom rest," said Viktor, "Go eat your cookies." He kissed Sonya on the head and sat in the other wicker chair. "Gloriana said you had a surprise planned?" He grinned, and she saw the goofy boy who brought a deck of UNO cards on their first date in case they ran out of things to talk about.

"Yes, she'll be bringing it out in a minute. I got us a tiramisu. Remember on our first date-"

"We went to that terrible Italian restaurant."

"And the waitress said-"

"Oh I forgot about her. Didn't she tell us we would-"

"Have eight children and be unhappy for the rest of our lives. Then she offered us a free slice of tiramisu to make up for our terrible futures."

They laughed at the memory. Of their younger selves giggling as the woman grabbed their palms and predicted nothing but intertwined lives of doom and gloom. Gloriana brought them each a slice of cake. Sonya took a bite, the sugar and coffee zipping straight to the pleasure center of her brain.

"Five kids and enjoying cake on the porch," said Viktor, scooping up a dollop of mascarpone on his fork. "I don't think that waitress was psychic."

"Yeah, we are not having eight children." Sonya laughed, then saw an opportunity. An opening. "Because when they take these babies out, I'm getting my tubes tied."

Viktor nodded. "Works for me."

"And we're keeping Gloriana. At least until the triplets are in school."

He nodded again, chewing on a lady finger, unaware of the monumental shift happening in his wife.

"And I want to go back to work. Not soon, but eventually. Part-time. Or get a hobby. Or volunteer. I haven't decided yet. Something that gets me out of the house a few times a week."

He looked at her slyly. "Sure, maybe you could-"

"I'm not learning how to golf." They both laughed, re-membering Viktor's disastrous attempts to lure Sonya into being his golfing buddy.

Was it that easy? No, the asking was easy. Agreeing to change while eating dessert on the porch high on Anniversary was easy. Making the changes would be harder.

Kane ran past on his evening jog, eyes forward, a grey-hound focused on the lure. Her stomach jumped. She felt the tiramisu coming back up but swallowed it.

Viktor played with a piece of hair that had escaped her updo. "How are you feeling?"

She said good.

A Man Goes On His First Date After His Wife Was Hanged For Witchcraft

Patience, I'm over here. I got us a table right by the fire. This place can get pretty busy after a witch-hanging. You look great, by the way. Sorry, I know coveting a woman's appearance is a sin, but the flogging I'll administer to myself tonight will be worth it to stare into your eyes. Your father tells me we have a lot in common. You lost your husband two years ago in a barn collapse, right? I've been there. I recently lost my wife. How recently? Hmm, an hour ago. Yes, it was my wife, Mary Bishop, that we just watched hang for witchcraft.

It's been a tough few months. From the first accusation, through testifying at her trial, to helping the reverend administer the witch test by throwing her in a river. Patience, I feel like I can be honest with you. Part of me wanted her to drown, just to prove everyone wrong. To prove that the woman who birthed my three children wasn't a loathsome witch. But, as we all saw, my wife Mary floated like a cork.

Do you have any relationship deal breakers? Mine would be if a woman has unsightly moles, her malevolent aura causes milk to spoil, or she has made a blood oath to the dark lord Satan. Also, short hair.

Yes, barkeep, we're ready to order. We'll have two thick ales and a roasted goose, head-on. You know Patience, they won't usually leave the head on the goose, but I'm a regular here at the Ingersoll Ordinary. I'm here every Wednesday for Bible Trivia. Every Friday for Bible Night. Every Saturday for Bible Bingo. Mary said I spent too much time here. She said I should be at home helping with chores and taking care of our six children. All that complaining was the first sign she was a witch. That, and her left-handedness.

Tell me about your ambitions. None? Great!

You have a hair on your collar. Ooh, a black one. Hopefully not from your black cat familiar who sneaks into your room at night, whispering tales of revenge in your oily ear. Kidding! It feels good to laugh.

Ok, yes, technically I arranged this date with your father before my wife was dead, but she's been locked away in Salem jail for weeks now. And you should know my wife cheated first, dancing naked in the moonlight with a half-man half-ram trying to conceive an heir to his throne in Hell. And me, stuck at home with only the fire to keep me company. Oh yes, and the nine children, sure.

Ahh, our goose is here. As you are the lady, I will allow you to enjoy the tender neck.

Listen, I know it looked bad, my wife spitting on me as they dragged her through the solemn throng of onlookers. I know she screamed that I only accused her of witchcraft because she wanted to learn how to read. Lies! Those falsehoods are as rotten as the potato she planted in the ground, causing Verity Davis to lose her infant son to the pox.

Let's play a game! It's called, would you rather. Tell me, would you rather spend an evening silently repairing the holes in your husband's clothing or laughing with your quilting friends about how your husband keeps ripping the seat of his pants?

Would you rather tell your husband he is the natural handsome leader of your household or that his profession as barber-surgeon was only given to him because his father sits on the church council?

Would you rather provide your husband with his eleventh child or ask to be spared from your wifely duty because you have been pregnant for over half of your life?

Patience, I know perfection cannot be achieved on Earth, and only in Heaven are we made divine by God's holy permission, but you're as close to perfect as God will allow a woman to be. Would you do me the honor of being my wife?

Wait, don't answer.
Your father already agreed.

And Now A Word From Our Sponsors

Penny Pinching Tips for the Morally Bankrupt is
brought to you by these fine businesses.

Crenshaw's Corn Dogs: The official concession of death row executions. Smell that delicious sizzle as you watch the light leave a possibly innocent man's eyes.

Perky Pete's Mini Golf: We have the deepest holes in town! Reach in to retrieve your ball and feel nothing but cold air. Deeper and deeper you'll stretch until you're pressed to the ground, your entire arm searching for your pitted plastic ball. Extend your arm until it hurts, splaying your fingers in the abyssal dark. You feel a brush of a hand on yours. Suddenly, the golf ball is wrapped in your clenched fist. You stand and vomit onto the Astroturf lawn. The last time you felt this sick was when a BMW narrowly missed hitting you in a crosswalk, making your life flash before your eyes. Buckle in! You've got seventeen holes to go!

Gianetto's Fine Italian Dining: Tomato free since '83

Rogard's Antiques: You break it, you buy it!

Rogard's Antiques: You touch it, you buy it!

Rogard's Antiques: You looked at your empty end table and thought it could use a vase or something so we snuck into your home, placed a vintage brass scale on your table, took your VISA out of your wallet, ran it through our mobile credit card reader, and charged you $250!

Shady Pines: The ONLY nursing home where EVERY resident is given a boomerang.

Six People See The Same Man And Derive Vastly Different Lessons From His Actions

Dan was sitting in the park holding a cardboard box that contained everything in his cubicle. From the Yankees tickets he had pinned to the wall, to the three KIND bars he kept in his top drawer. Ten years of life in that cube compacted into one cardboard square all in the name of downsizing.

The smell of hotdogs from a nearby cart tempted him, but he didn't have any cash on him and he doubted the $3 hotdog guy took Amex. A man in a plaid shirt stepped up to the cart and ordered a hotdog with mustard and relish. He sat at the opposite end of the bench and unwrapped the foil of his dog. From his Dockers pocket, he pulled a small shaker of rainbow sprinkles.

With a practiced motion, he doused the hotdog in sprinkles. Shaking and shaking until all traces of the interior contents were eclipsed by sugary bits. As he bit the end of the hotdog, sprinkles crunched in his teeth and sprayed all over his shirt. Watching the man devour the sprinkle-covered hotdog, Dan realized he could get through this. Sometimes, you have to bring your own positivity to a sour situation, until it turns into something sweet.

◆ ◆ ◆

Smooth jazz played over the Ruth's Chris Steakhouse speakers as the 16 oz. New York Strip glided toward its destination. Marvin peered out from the kitchen. He was usually too busy to watch customers receive their food, but whenever he had a spare moment, he loved to see their eyes get huge as they were served the delicious meal he had prepared for them.

This steak was headed for a table of two. A middle-aged couple in a corner booth. When their food arrived, the wife smiled and dug into her crab cakes. The man frowned at his steak. What was wrong? Marvin had cooked it to a perfect medium rare. The man pulled a jar of neon jimmies from his pocket. He dumped the entire jar onto the steak while his wife pretended to admire the steakhouse's ceiling tiles. Marvin's dad was right. He should go to law school.

❖ ❖ ❖

As she plunked away at her novel (6,000 words down, 64,000 to go), sipping her $6 latte, Jia got a text from Samra.

Hey beautiful! Wanna get away this weekend? A friend has a place in Michigan we can use. Near a lake!!!

She'd been seeing Samra for three months, so a weekend trip wasn't out of the question. But it was Thursday. Jia would have to find someone to feed her cat and she was supposed to give her roommate a ride to Costco on Sunday and she'd need to pack and...

A man tapped her on the shoulder.

"Are you using this chair?"

"No, go at it."

The man sat in the chair next to her. He set down his cup of coffee and pulled from his pocket a small jar of red, white, and green nonpareils. He unscrewed the lid and dumped the entire jar into his mug. With a wooden coffee stirrer, he swirled the steaming sludge, then gulped it down in two swallows, like a duck with a hoagie roll.

Fuck it. If that man had the courage to put nonpareils in his coffee in public, then Jia could take one spontaneous trip to Michigan.

She texted Samra back, *yes.*

◆ ◆ ◆

Kayla had encountered her share of weirdos working at the AMC snack counter, but the man who asked for his popcorn tub half full so he could fill the other half with sprinkles was in a class of his own. As she watched him glop imitation butter all over the sugary mess, her dinner rose in her throat. She ran to the bathroom and vomited. That was it. Tomorrow she was scheduling her abortion.

◆ ◆ ◆

There's no point in living any longer. As Noah stood on the ledge on the roof of his apartment building, he contemplated his life. In vet school, they taught him that quality of life was most important in deciding which animals to put down. If he was a dog, his owners would have shot him full of pentobarbital long ago.

Noah looked across the street into the building across from him. He saw a woman mopping, kids wrestling, a man adding powdered cheese to a pot of Kraft macaroni. He watched him stir in milk and butter, salt and pepper, then he grabbed a container of chocolate sprinkles and dumped them in. He tasted a spoonful of the brown macaroni, shook his head, and added a handful of purple-colored sugar. He took another bite, and nodded, satisfied with his creation.

If this monster could take up oxygen in this world, by God, Noah should too. He stepped back off the ledge. He would live.

◆ ◆ ◆

It was Fan's first day at SunCo Systems. All morning she had been signing paperwork and watching poorly acted videos about how to confront workplace disasters. At noon, Yara from

HR said she could join her for lunch in the break room. Fan grabbed her sandwich from the fridge and sat with Yara and a man with a plaid tie.

"Dale Evans, IT Manager," he said as he shook her hand. He took the lid off of his Caesar salad and took a bite.

"Dale, aren't you forgetting something?" whispered Yara as she prodded a jar across the table.

"Oh, thanks." Dale poured Halloween sprinkles, white skulls, black cats, and orange pumpkins all over his salad.

That decided it. Fan was going to burn her mother's house to the ground.

A Woman Gives A Description To A Sketch Artist Of The Rapscallion Stealing Pies Off Her Windowsill

Thank you for taking the time to make this drawing for me Mr. Cooper. I'm at the end of my rope with this boy. Every time I leave a pie to cool on my windowsill this dessert loving reprobate snatches it right off. I've called the law on him, but he hides in the woods every time Sheriff Paxton comes to grab him. I keep thinking he'll move on to another farm or back to where he came from, but he's a locust without a swarm. An eighty-pound plague. I swear, I'm this close to putting sheep's blood above my door.

He's a white boy, about four foot five, maybe twelve years old. He wears a straw hat and filthy overalls. His front teeth are missing. I can't be sure if they fell out naturally or rotted away from the ungodly amount of sugar he consumes.

His eyes? Beady, searching, like two greased cherries rolling in his sockets. Instead of pupils, could you draw the silhouettes of pies with a tendril of steam rising from the top? It'll give a good sense of what this animal's aims are.

Mouth? The lips are smiling. The coy grin of a boy who knows where his next dessert is coming from. The mouth is large enough that he could eat all the filling from a peach pie in two gulps, leaving you with an empty pie shell spinning in your windowsill.

Face shape? Three months ago I would have said, hollow, hungry, with the prideful eyes of a boy who will refuse a woman's kind offer a slice of apple pie, then wait until her back is turned to steal the whole pie off her windowsill. Now, he's as plump as a Christmas hog. A neck with a ring of lard so thick it overflows his collar. Cheeks like a chipmunk with mumps.

Hair? Black as pitch with a dozen cowlicks, each one resembling a horn of the devil. Thick as a bramble patch and slippery as a greased viper. The type of hair it seems you have a firm grasp of as you're chasing him across your lawn as he carries off your pecan pie, but with one twist of his neck, he's wriggled out of your grasp, taking your dessert with him.

Ears? Enormous. Two empty pie tins sticking out from the sides of his head. Ears so big they can hear the moment you leave your kitchen to read a book in the living room. But not so big that they can hear you screaming from your window violently shaking a rolling pin.

Hands? Fingers like overstuffed sausages. Covered in thick calluses, rendering them impervious to even the hottest pie dishes straight from a four hundred degree oven.

Nose? A snout with nostrils large enough to fit a whole cherry. So that when you chase the mongrel into the woods and discover him blue in the face, with cherries choking his breathing tubes, you make him promise that if you save his miserable life he'll never steal another pie from you again. And even after you thump him on the back and he swears on his mama's grave he'll never bother you again, you find him that very night sneaking out of your kitchen window, a peanut butter icebox pie under his deceitful little arm.

I have a sample of his handwriting if that will help. Here's a note that says *No mor starabery*. He slipped it under my door after I made a strawberry pie and he threw it up in my hydrangeas.

Mr. Cooper, that sounds like you're blaming the victim, telling me I should cool my pies somewhere other than an easily accessible first-floor windowsill. Why should I have to change my routine on account of the criminal actions of a sweet-toothed roughneck? Next, I suppose you'll ask what I was wearing to invite the animal's vile behavior. For your information, it was an apron. A long one.

Thank you for your drawing, Mr. Cooper. I'm going to

show it around the businesses on Main Street. See if anyone recognizes the pie-snatching miscreant. Probably head to Day's Pharmacy first. Say, do you know if they sell rat poison?

Very Easy Would You Rathers

Would you rather have feet for hands or hands for hands?

Would you rather have spaghetti for hair or spaghetti for dinner?

Would you rather fight a hundred duck-sized horses or drink lemonade in a hammock?

Would you rather have an arm growing out of the back of your head or an arm growing out of your shoulder as you take part in a pioneering limb regrowth study?

Would you rather get murdered by a serial killer or be married to one, but he's a nice family man and of course you're horrified when you find out what he's done, but no one suspects you had anything to do with it and Florence Pugh plays you in the movie version?

Would you rather always be wearing wet socks or publish a bestselling book of poems at age thirty-two?

Would you rather kill your best friend or have your best friend kill it in an air guitar tournament?

Would you rather be in jail for twenty years for a crime you didn't commit or get no jail time for a crime you did commit?

Would you rather have a head the size of a grapefruit or a grapefruit the size of a head?

Would you rather have a girl's night out with Oprah and Gayle or a girl's night in with Melania Trump and the ghost of Eva Braun?

Would you rather live in the world of Harry Potter, but be a muggle, or live in the world of Twilight, but be a coat rack?

Would you rather be a white man or anything else?

Makeout Point

Dorothy's legs sweated under the thick felt of her pink poodle skirt. She wished she could pull it up, exposing her legs to the cool breeze coming in from the open car window, but she wouldn't want to give Buck Hammond, captain of the football team, the wrong idea. Which was simply the right idea, too soon. Buck drove them down the dark highway in his dad's Bel Air, going too fast around every curve. Dorothy had told her parents she was studying for a geometry test at her best friend Lucy Paget's house, and she hoped her mom didn't get the bright idea to call Lucy's mother to check on her story.

"Almost there," said Buck, one hand on the wheel, one hand holding hers. "PJ told me about this quiet spot where he takes all the girls. Of course, I've never been before."

Liar, thought Dorothy. Buck Hammond had played backseat bingo with half the girls at Midland High and a quarter of their mothers. But tonight was her turn, and she was going to make the most of it. Once word spread that she'd spread for Buck Hammond there would be no more whispers of Frigid Dorothy, Dorothy the Square, Never Even Had A Kiss Dorothy. Sure, other girls, like Rosemary Watson, with their slick smiles and tight sweaters, would still make fun of her frizzy black hair and stubby legs. But by hooking up with Buck, she could at least remove this, the largest target on her back.

"This must be it." Buck slowed at a sign that read:

Makeout Point
One mile East

Underneath the words, two cartoon rabbits with hearts in their eyes kissed, their tiny rabbit tongues knotted together.

"That sign's grody," said Dorothy.

Buck shrugged his wide shoulders and turned onto the road into the forest. "PJ's hip. If he says it's fat city, I'll trust him."

They drove into the dark, the Bel Air's headlights showing them nothing but tree-lined road. Dorothy stared out the window, mentally unhooking her own bra to make sure her fingers didn't fumble with the hooks when the time came. Nailed to a tree up ahead, she saw a second sign that said:

Makeout Point
Rated #14 Spot for Necking in 1952 by Backseat Magazine

"But why advertise being number fourteen?" she wondered aloud.

"What's that baby?" asked Buck. The further they drove into the forest, the huskier his voice became. He rubbed his hand up and down her thigh, trying to get under her skirt, but impeded by the thick sweaty felt.

"Nothing," said Dorothy, "Just... what the?" It was a banner, suspended across the road.

Makeout Point
By passing under this banner you consent to
be photographed by the proprietor.
Free official Makeout Point fedoras to first fifty entrants.
Ten days since last mountain lion attack.

What type of make out spot gave away hats? Were mountain lions common in Michigan? And who would photograph her? She looked over at Buck's handsome silhouette. Was this an elaborate joke? Was he planning to get her to take off her top, then have twenty of her classmates pop out of the woods to point and laugh? He'd seemed sincere when he asked her out, even though Dorothy knew he'd only done it because she'd been sitting next to his ex-girlfriend at the football game and Buck was trying to make her jealous.

"Buck, I'm not so sure about this place," said Dorothy.

"Damn it, Dorothy," said Buck, letting go of her thigh,

"Everyone told me you were a real icebox bitch, but I thought I'd give you a chance."

"No Buck, it's not you, it's this place. Aren't you reading the signs?" She pointed to a square sign to their right that said:

Makeout Point
The lens of the human eye is the size of an M&M.

"Who cares about some dumb old signs?" He accelerated down the rest of the road and screeched to a stop in a clearing. The view was gorgeous, the trees opening up to a panorama of the entire town. The stars twinkled overhead, and the full moon shone bright and lovely. There were seven cars in the clearing and Buck parked in between a Cadillac and a Thunderbird, both with windows too fogged to see who was inside.

Buck turned off the car and leaned toward her. This was it. She was doing it. Parking. With a real live boy. Without asking, he untucked her sweater and slid a hand up her shirt, pawing at her breast. He leaned toward her. Her first kiss. Oh god, did her breath smell? Was she doing this right? His mouth engulfed the entire bottom half of her face and he rubbed his hard crotch on her thigh. Through the sliver of window behind him, Dorothy saw another sign.

Makeout Point
$15/minute

Dorothy was about to warn Buck that his clumsy humping was costing them a small fortune when he grunted. Wetness leaked through his trousers, staining the face of her felt poodle. That was a stain she wouldn't ask for mother's help to remove. Buck heaved himself off of her as she tucked her sweater back in. It surprised her how quick it had been. How easy it was to be easy.

Buck had a blissful grin on his face. Dorothy relaxed. She must not have been too bad if he'd gotten his satisfaction that quickly. On Monday morning, Buck would tell everyone what he and Dorothy had done. No one would call her frigid after an evening with Buck. Maybe she'd be able to leverage this new-found loose reputation into a date with a boy she actually liked.

They watched the stars for a bit, neither wanting to hear the sound of the other's voice. Dorothy thought more about the odd signs. It must be a practical joke, like when Drew Swenson had written "Don't" on all the STOP signs in town.

"So," said Buck, putting the keys in the ignition.

"Thanks," said Dorothy.

"My pleasure." It literally had been.

Tinny calliope music played from somewhere in the trees. Dorothy looked out the window, but it was too dark to see where it was coming from. She'd completed her mission of getting with Buck. Now she wanted him to drive her away from this creepy place. But at the sound of the calliope music, Buck took the keys out of the ignition and cocked his head as though waiting for further instructions.

"Buck, what's happening?" she asked, but he held up a finger to quiet her.

She was about to protest his shushing when a loud voice yelled, "Ladies switch."

"That means you," said Buck, leaning over to push open her door.

"What?" shouted Dorothy over the circus music, which was growing louder and more frantic. Her question was answered when a blur of blonde hair and purple velvet dragged her out of the car, threw her to the ground, and took her seat in the car with Buck. Dorothy lay stunned in the mud as girls ran around the clearing, trying to find an empty car. As the last car door slammed, Dorothy caught her breath.

"We have a winner," said the loud voice, which came from a speaker perched in a tree. "Would the young lady in the pink skirt please come to the manager's office to collect her prize?"

What was going on? Everyone else had known what to do, as if they had had a rulebook in their pockets. None of her friends had ever mentioned getting shoved out of a car while necking with a boy. But then again, Dorothy only had one real friend, and Lucy was as much a capital-V virgin as she was. Lucy had been so excited to see Buck slip his arm around Dorothy's shoulders after the football game that she'd volunteered a cover story to tell Dorothy's parents. Lucy was a hopeless romantic, reading every Jane Lambert romance novel and Seventeen magazine she could get her hands on. That Buck, the brooding hunk, had secret feelings for Dorothy, the plain Jane, fit perfectly into her rose-tinted view of the world.

Dorothy stood up, squelching out of the mud and wiping her hands on her ruined skirt. Inside the car, Buck and the blonde were already making out. She'd be lying if she said it didn't sting to be replaced so easily. Simply an interchangeable girl-shaped mammal. Though she knew Buck was so out of her league they were playing different sports, it had been nice to feel wanted. His eyes on her breasts, his hand on her thigh, his lips on hers. She indulged in a moment of self-pity. Her mission had been to sully her squeaky clean reputation, which she had accomplished. As long as Buck gave her a ride back into town, she didn't care where else his tongue went.

Hidden by the trees and illuminated by a single light on a tall post, she spotted a small green shed with the sign *Makeout Point Manager's Office* above a window with a counter. She struggled toward it, her Mary Janes getting sucked into the mud with every step. A middle-aged man in a yellow and black pinstripe suit with a lily tucked behind his ear grinned in the moonlight. He looked like a gangster on vacation. As Dorothy stepped up to the window, she saw the small shack had a bed and a griddle where three pancakes bubbled, ready to be turned.

"And what is your name, young lady?" asked the man. His voice was silky smooth like a radio announcer selling laundry detergent.

"Your pancakes are burning."

"Is that Polish... oh, gee." He turned and saw his pancakes smoking, then grabbed a spatula from the dirt floor and flipped the pancakes onto a plate.

"Thanks." He put the plate on his bed then stood back at the window. "Now, what is your name?"

"First, I have some questions about this place. What are the-"

He cut her off, pointing at a sign that said:

Makeout Point Rules
  1. No Questions

"That's the only rule? I can't ask questions?" Dorothy felt more and more that she had entered another universe where all the rules she'd been taught about how to live in a polite society no longer applied. In *Makeout Point* they wore gloves on their feet and always ate with their elbows on the table. "But why..."

The man pointed again at the sign. "What's your name, darling?"

"Oh, so you can ask questions, but I-" she said, then stopped. Getting angry would not make any of this easier to figure out. She considered running back to Buck's car and demanding he drive her home. But the man in the pinstripe suit spoke with such authority. Dorothy wasn't used to defying adults, and she wasn't about to start with this mysterious man in the middle of the woods. "My name is Dorothy Speer. I'm sixteen years old. I live at 3803 Concord Street with my mother Lorna, a homemaker, my father John, an accountant, and my brother, Mike, an eighth-grader."

Though it was more information than he had asked for, the man wrote everything in a spiral-bound notebook. "And what brings you to *Makeout Point* this evening?"

"Um, it's in the name, isn't it?"

The man sighed. "Yes, but more specifically. Why did you, Dorothy Speer, come to *Makeout Point*?" he said, his tone implying there could be a wrong answer.

"That's not any of your business."

He tapped the sign again. A second rule had appeared.

Makeout Point Rules

   1. No Questions
   2. All Questions Must Be Answered

Dorothy looked at the cars parked in a row behind her. No open windows. Even so, she leaned in and lowered her voice. "I wanted to make out with Buck Hammond so the girls at school would stop saying I'm frigid."

"Of course. A perfectly good reason," said the man, nodding in a satisfied manner, "As the winner of this year's *Make-out Point Shuffle,* you have your choice of prizes." He flipped through pages in his notebook. The smell of pancakes made Dorothy's eyes water. Her mom made pancakes every Sunday when they came home from church. She wished she was back home, tucked under her floral quilt right now.

"But how am I the winner?" She paused. "When I have played musical chairs in the past, the person left out is the loser."

The man grinned. "You're no longer stuck in a car getting groped by a boy you don't like so girls won't whisper about you in the locker room. Seems like a win for you. Anyway, here are this year's prizes." He ripped a page from the notebook and handed it to her.

   Makeout Point Shuffle Grand Prizes
   1. A year supply of SPAM pork products
   2. The ability to talk to birds
   3. $100,000
   4. The death of Henry Kissinger

"Who is-?" she started to ask. But even if she knew, she wouldn't kill someone. She also ruled out the year of SPAM. Her dad had developed a taste for it during the war, and she shuddered at a full year of smelly SPAM sandwiches packed in her lunchbox. The $100,000 was the obvious choice, but she bet there was a catch like they pay you in nickels or most of it gets taken by taxes. The ability to talk to birds was intriguing for a moment. Then she realized it was a gag prize, like the X-Ray

Specs her brother ordered from the back of his Superman comics.

The man chewed on his dry pancakes, watching her pore over the prize choices. A revving engine startled them both as the Cadillac pulled out of *Makeout Point* and drove down the road to the highway. Watching the car leave, containing its driver and whatever girl had jumped in with him, a shiver went up her spine, making her whole scalp tighten. If there were eight couples and eight cars, how had she gotten left out? Where had the ninth girl come from?

"Where..." she started, then stopped when the man tapped the sign, his mouth too full of pancake to speak. Three tears leaked from Dorothy's right eye.

"Don't cry sweetie," said the man, mopping her tear with a pancake then taking a bite, "Killing Kissinger will save a lot of lives."

"I want to go home," sobbed Dorothy.

"It's too late for that." The man nodded toward Buck's taillights, as he drove the Bel Air back down the narrow road.

Dorothy sprinted after the car, screaming for him to stop. She'd jam herself in the trunk if it meant a ride home. But either Buck didn't see her or he didn't care because the Bel Air sped down the dirt path, spraying Dorothy with even more mud. There were five cars left in the clearing. If there had been eight cars and two had left, where was the missing car? Maybe it had pulled out in front of Buck. Or she'd counted wrong. Either way, this was her chance to get out of here. She ran over to a blue Pontiac and banged on the driver's side window, fogged by hot breath on the chilly night until the driver rolled it down a smidge.

"What!" yelled the boy. She recognized him from the basketball team. His name was Dave or Don or...

"Danny, please, I need a ride back into town."

"Can't you leave with the guy you came with?"

"No, Buck drove away. Please, I'll do your algebra homework for a month."

Danny rolled the window all the way down. Dorothy could see the interrupted couple lit by the full moon. Danny was in his t-shirt and boxer shorts, red lipstick smeared around his mouth. The girl in the passenger seat leaned forward to look at Dorothy. It was Rosemary Watson, the originator of the nickname Frigid Dorothy.

"Is that you, Dorothy?" said Rosemary, a wicked grin on her perfect face. "Did I hear that Buck Hammond left you behind?"

"No, no… he didn't… we did," Dorothy stammered. She had wanted everyone at school to know she had gotten with Buck Hammond. Now everyone at school would know she was the girl Buck Hammond had left behind.

"No wonder," said Rosemary, "One touch and you probably froze his Johnson off." Rosemary cackled as Danny rolled up his window.

Dorothy stood still, sinking deeper into the muddy ground. She reached out a hand to knock on the window of the green car to her left, but she couldn't bring herself to do it. The shame of explaining her pitiful situation to another gloating couple was too much for her to take.

All she had wanted was to make out with a boy and tell everyone about it. And all she had done was to give herself an even worse reputation at school and win an idiotic contest where the rules kept changing. If Buck was gone and getting a ride from someone else wasn't an option, her only choice was to go back to the man in the shack. Maybe if she went along with his game, he'd take her home. He had to have a car. How else would he have gotten the ingredients for those pancakes all the way out here in the forest?

She trudged through the soft ground to the manager's shack. The man in the pinstripe suit was spooning more batter onto the griddle.

"Did your friends refuse to give you a ride?" He put on a fake frown.

"They aren't my friends."

"The way you slunk back here like a cat whose tail got caught in a furnace told me that, Dorothy dear," he said, smiling. Dorothy noticed his teeth didn't have any gaps, one solid row of tooth on top, one on bottom. "Dear girl, you still haven't told me what prize you want. But take your time. You've got a whole year until the next *Makeout Point Shuffle*."

"Are you expecting me to stay out here in the forest for the next year with you?" Dorothy's organs vibrated with rage. She kicked the flimsy shed with her muddy shoes. "My father does taxes for the mayor. You can't keep me hostage. My friend Lucy knew I was coming out here with Buck. She'll come looking for me when I don't come home."

"You're making a lot of assumptions there." But he didn't contradict any of them. Again, the homey smell of the pancakes made tears trickle down her face. She missed her house. Her family. Her Lucy. She never should have gotten in the car with Buck. Right now she should be sitting in Lucy's bedroom eating a giant bowl of buttery popcorn and giggling every time Lucy's mother came in to ask the girls to quiet down.

As Dorothy stood in the moonlight, regretting every action that led her to this moment, the man flipped all three pancakes onto a paper plate and put it on the counter between them. "Eat."

"No." Her family had gone to see *Alice in Wonderland* last year at the drive-in. She remembered when Alice had eaten the cake that had made her grow enormous. No way was she eating these pancakes.

"The last thing you ate today was an apple from your mom's fruit bowl at 3 pm."

"No." She flipped the plate into the dirt and stomped the pancakes into the mud.

The man frowned, rubbing the petals of the lily behind his ear. "You're rather ungrateful for a girl who's won a big prize."

"Oh right, the big prize I get for getting shoved into the mud and abandoned in a forest." Two more cars pulled out of the clearing. Dorothy waved at their taillights disappearing into the dark. "Bye-bye Pete or Jimmy or whoever else gets to leave this *damned* place tonight." The curse left her mouth tingling. She turned back to the man. "I don't want your money or your birds or your *fucking* SPAM."

"So you want the fourth prize?" He picked up his notebook to mark down her choice.

"Yes, I want the fourth prize." It didn't matter what she chose. This was all a joke, anyway.

"Very well then." The man made an exaggerated check mark on the paper and winked.

The sun was setting over Boston. Men drove home from office buildings to wives with Franks & Beans simmering on the stove. At Fenway, Dom DiMaggio ran toward home base to give the Red Sox a lead over the Yankees. And over the Charles River at Harvard, the nation's best and brightest read Kierkegaard, argued about Eisenhower, and quoted *I Love Lucy's* Vitameatavegamin episode long into the night.

The most peculiar figure in Boston that evening was a girl covered in mud, standing in the shadows of the Harvard Quad. She was hidden behind a gigantic statue of a seated man holding a book whose left toe shined gold from years of good luck rubs. Around her were large red brick buildings framing an open field of grass. Scattered young people walked on the paths, no one noticing the girl hidden in the shadows. The breeze swept her hair into her face. When she raised her right hand to push it back, she found she was holding a small silver revolver.

"How about Cronin's?" asked a young blonde man in a brown suit. He turned to his companion, a black haired man with a dour expression. They paused in front of the statue.

"That place is a dump," said the other man in a thick European accent.

His friend sighed. "That's the point, Henry. You won't find cheap beer at someplace that isn't."

Every hair on Dorothy's body stood up straight. She was

here to redeem her prize. It hadn't been a joke. The man in the shack had transported her through time and space, put a gun in her hand, and expected her to pull the trigger. Her pulse thudded in her ears. She might faint. Her body swayed backward, but her feet were glued to the sidewalk.

No no no. She tried to scream. To alert the man. To get him to run away, out of range of whatever she was about to do. But all that came out was a thin rasp. Maybe this wasn't real. Maybe it was a dream put into her head by the man in the pinstripe suit. Maybe she wasn't about to take a man's life.

Henry made a show of taking off his glasses, cleaning them with a handkerchief, then placing them back on his face. "Fine. But you're driving."

"Great." His friend patted his pockets. "Oh shit, I left my wallet in the classroom. Wait here. I'll be back in a jiff." The blonde man jogged into the darkness, leaving Henry alone. He pulled a newspaper out of his briefcase, tried reading it in the dimming light, then jammed it back inside. He checked his watch, mumbling in a language Dorothy didn't understand.

As if controlled by marionette strings, Dorothy stepped out of the darkness. Her right arm raised, no longer under her mind's control. Her feet rushed toward Henry Kissinger, stopping when the gun nestled at the base of his skull. He jumped at the cold metal pressed to the back of his neck. Dorothy's finger pulled the trigger. The bang made her ears ring. Blood splattered her white blouse and dripped down her face. A dribble from her nose dropped on to her tongue, hot and metallic.

Henry thunked onto the sidewalk like a slab of beef falling off a countertop. Blood gushed from the wound in his neck. He gurgled and twitched for a moment, then went still. Dorothy retched bile; thankful she'd refused the pancakes. The pool of blood expanded until it surrounded Dorothy's shoes. She took a step back, now in control of her body.

Who had she killed? Was he a devoted father? A loyal brother? A cherished son? Murder was a mortal sin. She was a cold-blooded killer like the Nazis she'd seen in newsreels. And she'd chosen this. For the rest of her days, she would know she'd chosen to take a man's life rather than eat SPAM for a year. That made her worse than a Nazi. Her skin flushed, reacting to the blazing tendrils of hellfire reaching up to drag her into eternal damnation.

"Oh my god! Henry," shouted the blonde man who had returned from retrieving his wallet. He knelt next to Henry's limp body, checking for a pulse that had already stopped. "Miss, did you see who did this?"

Dorothy shook her head.

The blonde man took in her bloody clothes, shell shocked expression, and finally the gun still clutched in her right hand. "Oh...you, but… POLICE!"

Dorothy ran. Sprinting down the sidewalk, no idea where she was headed. Behind her, she heard the man continue to shout for someone to call the police. He'd seen her. He'd tell the police what she looked like, that is, if they didn't find her themselves. A girl covered in blood running down the street with a gun in her hand was bound to be stopped. Should she turn herself in? Would they give a teen girl the electric chair? Or would she spend the rest of her days locked in a tiny cell?

As she turned a corner she tripped, bracing herself for impact on the hard pavement. Instead, her arms plunged into soft mud. One car was left in the clearing, a beige Ford sedan. It was close to midnight, the full moon straight above her in the sky. The only sounds were crickets and frogs screaming for a mate. Dorothy stood and wobbled toward the manager's shack. Adrenaline made her blood pump so hard it felt like her entire body was getting squeezed in a vise.

"Welcome back!" shouted the man as she approached the window. He handed her a blue bath towel. "Clean yourself up."

She tried to take the towel, but the gun was stuck in her hand as though it had fused to her palm. The man took her hand, pried her fingers apart, and slipped the gun into his breast pocket. Then he wiped the splatters of blood and mud from her face and handed her the towel to take care of her arms and legs.

"Put this on," he said as he handed her a silver sash. In big black letters it said *Makeout Point Shuffle Queen 1953.*

"Did I really...?" she started to ask, before the man tapped the *No Questions* sign.

"But, to answer you, yes, you did kill Henry Kissinger. And no, I don't think the police will connect the murder of an academic in Boston to a sixteen-year-old girl in Midland, Michigan."

She nodded. Her crime was already feeling further away. Her brain fuzzing the details. Back in the reality of the forest clearing, the man bleeding out on the sidewalk was a bad dream.

The bang of a car door slamming echoed through the clearing. A husky boy wearing huge black glasses and a thick argyle sweater stumbled away from the Ford toward the Manager's Office. He looked as awful as Dorothy felt, shaking and sweating with skin tinged with green under his freckles.

"Oh yes, I forgot! Dorothy Speer meet Chester Blumenthal, our 1953 *Makeout Point Shuffle King.*" The man in the pinstripe suit waved the boy forward and handed him a sash.

Dorothy had been wrong. There hadn't been an extra girl, but a boy who had been left alone. The boy wasn't handsome, with dishwater blonde hair and teeth too large for his mouth. He took asthmatic gasps, as if he had just run ten miles. What prize had he chosen?

Chester put on the sash with trembling hands. He looked her up and down. "Are you all right?"

"Yes," she said, surprised how steady her voice was. She was trapped in an irrational nightmare and had killed a man, but all things considered, she was all right.

"Are you bleeding?"

"Oh that! It's not mine." She was saved from having to answer whose blood it was, when the man in the pinstripe suit took out a bulky black camera with a large silver flashbulb from behind the counter. "Scooch together, you two."

Dorothy and Chester stood pressed at the shoulder, looking like two dolls beaten up and jammed together by a violent toddler.

"Jelly and cheese!" said the man as the camera flashed. "We're all set. I have your information, you've both redeemed your prizes, and I took your picture for the official *Makeout Point* scrapbook. You are free to go." The man took hold of a metal grate at the top of the counter's window and pulled it down.

"No," Dorothy shouted, sticking her arms under the grate. "You can't do that! You can't do these things to us and not offer any explanation. What do the signs mean? How long has this place existed? Who did I-" She stopped, not wanting to reveal to Chester which prize she had chosen.

"Hmm, so many questions," said the man, smiling his un-gapped smile, "I suppose I could bend the rules and answer, but I'd need something in return."

"What do you want?" She'd give anything, do anything, to have this night make sense. For this jagged piece to fit smoothly into the pattern of her life.

Before the man could answer, Chester grabbed Dorothy by the arm and dragged her toward his car. She screamed and tried to wriggle free, but he grabbed her around the waist and stuck a sweaty palm over her mouth.

"Don't you wanna get out of here? Do you think that man is going to give you any actual answers? Huh? Do you?"

The boy was right. The safer path was letting questions go unanswered. She allowed Chester to lead her to his car. He opened the passenger door for her. Before she got in, she looked back toward the manager's shack, but all she saw was a single white lily growing out of the mud.

"Chester look, it's gone!"

"Good," he replied and gestured for her to get in the car.

She got in. He ran around to the driver's side, jammed the keys in the ignition, and whipped out of the clearing. As the narrow road twisted and turned, he was forced to slow down or risk running them off the road. The signs she'd read on her way into *Makeout Point* had writing on the back.

Now Leaving Makeout Point
Was it something we said?

The rabbits who had been attached at the tongue now held up their thumbs, hitchhiking with bright green hobo bindles over their shoulders. Dorothy was about to point out the signs to Chester, when he turned to her and said, "I took the money."

Liar, thought Dorothy. Chester Blumenthal had done something terrible. Something that was eating him up from the inside out. The kind thing to do would be to divulge her own crime, but Dorothy couldn't bring herself to say the words, as though saying it out loud might change it from a hazy half-dream into a solid reality.

Makeout Point
If he had lived, Henry Kissinger would have committed war crimes in Vietnam, Bangladesh, Chile, Cyprus and East Timor. The human capacity for evil is larger than all the M&Ms in the world.

Was this true? Was the man she killed destined for a life of evil?

In the whole strange evening, the one part that confused her most was the man in the pinstripe suit's insistence that she told him the real reason she came to *Makeout Point*. Was he trying to teach her a lesson? Or was Dorothy trying to extract purpose from a terrifying, nonsensical series of events?

Makeout Point
Man will walk on the Moon in 1969. Dial MO-6253 to order an official Makeout Point Moon Landing cardigan.

A man on the Moon? It was something out of a science fiction movie. Presumably the sign was meant for Chester. His shoulders relaxed, and he released a shuddering breath.

Here she was again. In a car with a boy headed down a dark road. On Monday, it would be back to school for bullies to call her loser, square, frigid. But could a loser have taken out a war criminal? Would a square have kept her cool while confronted with a mysterious man with no gaps between his teeth? And if she was so frigid, why was she wearing a skirt that, underneath the blood and mud, bore a stain of Buck's pleasure?

As they reached the end of the forest road and pulled onto the highway, Dorothy saw a final sign.

Makeout Point
Who are you? Wouldn't you like to know?

A Lady's Guide To Death

Ladies! We're all going to die! However, just because we must all succumb to the inevitable decay of time doesn't mean we can stop conforming to patriarchal expectations for even one millisecond. Follow this simple guide to make sure you maintain your ladylike charms even as your body putrefies.

How To Die

The top three most attractive ways for women to die are:

1. From consumption, scarlet fever, or any disease that makes you thin and waiflike but allows you to keep all of your hair.
2. Getting killed violently in order to inspire a man's future heroic actions.
3. Timing an aneurysm so you're wearing sexy lingerie and keel over into a pool of rose petals.

Where To Die

When choosing where to die, make sure it inconveniences as few people as possible. (e.g. in your bed, in an Uber on the way to a funeral home, already in a grave). A good rule of thumb: If your death causes anyone grief, you're doing it wrong!

When To Die

A lady may die tragically young and gorgeous or contentedly old and withered, having given every ounce of herself to her husband, children, and grandchildren. Anything in between is wrong.

Why To Die

A lot of this is out of your control, but the ideal death for a lady is smoke inhalation from a fire started by a faulty oven while baking an apple pie. The lady sheroically saves her six children (all natural births) from the flames, singing her apron in a gently sexy way. She then collapses softly on the lawn after demanding the paramedics help her children before her. Bonus points if she also saves the pie.

Your Last Will & Testament

In your will, bequeath everything to your husband. If you die unmarried, leave everything to a charity. Something with animals, but only cute ones. Remember to clearly label every single item in your home with its intended recipient to prevent discord among family members. Don't create drama from beyond the grave!

Your Funeral

Choose a date for your funeral that works with everyone's schedule and won't spoil future holidays with the memory of your death. A lady's funeral should be tasteful, yet erotic. The flowers should be white roses. The food should be chocolate cheesecake. The music should be anything by The Pussycat Dolls. Pre-book the caterer, florist, and musicians. Once you've put your deposits down, you MUST die before your planned funeral, so choose a date wisely.

Your Burial Method

There are three acceptable ways for a lady's body to be preserved.

1. Buried in a sexy casket. (Hot pink wood, red velvet interior, two humps on top to indicate boobs)
2. Cremated and then your ashes are pressed into a big shiny gem that is placed on a tasteful tiara and worn by your most beautiful daughter.
3. Burial at sea. Everyone looks sexy wet. As your bikini-clad corpse sinks into the drink, your guests can party in international waters.

Your Obituary

Have a photo chosen already so you don't get stuck with

an unflattering picture from your best frenemy's bachelorette party in Nashville where you're swallowing your own vomit. Also, have your obituary pre-written. Feel free to fudge some details such as your age, weight, and how much you actually volunteered at that soup kitchen.

If You Become A Ghost

If your spirit is doomed to walk the Earth until the end of time, choose the location you haunt wisely. Too many women choose to vengefully haunt their ex-boyfriend's home. Maybe your ex killed you and got away with it, but haunting his condo makes you seem desperate. Not a good look for eternity. Instead, haunt a more ladylike location such as a tearoom, spa, or Sephora.

If You Go To Heaven

Congratulations! You were a good girl on Earth. Here are three tips for your eternal reward.

1. White is not flattering on everyone. Ask if you can get robes in cream or ivory.
2. Find your husband. If you have died before him, wait patiently for his arrival before enjoying any element of Heavenly glory.
3. Be helpful! Don't sit on your cloud all day. Ask God if he needs any tidying done, meatloaves made, or shelves Swiffered.

If You Go To Hell

Yikes! Hope that abortion was worth it.

If There Is No Afterlife

Luxuriate in the never-ending expanse of the universe, released from the constraints and expectations that plagued your life. You're free!

Smucker's Fruit Spread Gift Guide

This year, instead of giving your loved one a boring old bouquet, give them the sweetest gift of all, a jar of Smucker's delicious fruit spreads. With over twenty flavors to choose from, you'll be able to tell that special someone exactly what you mean.

Strawberry Jam: Enduring Love

Strawberry Jelly: New Love

Strawberry Preserves: Please take me back, I'm so sorry for sleeping with your sister.

Grape Jelly: Undying Friendship

Grape Jam: Undying Enmity

Apple Jelly: Hey, did you know there is such a thing as Apple Jelly?

Blackberry Jam: You have a secret admirer and it is me, the person who just handed you a jar of blackberry jam.

Raspberry Jam: You won't see me again.

Raspberry Jelly: You won't see me again until you least expect it.

Natural Red Tart Cherry Fruit Spread: Please vaccinate my grandchildren.

Apricot Preserves: Will you marry me?

Blueberry Preserves: Will you divorce me?

Cherry Preserves: Please stop being so difficult about custody. We brought these kids into the world and they deserve to have both parents in their lives. I know I was gone a lot, but only because I was working so hard to build a future for us.

Pineapple Preserves: You're a great mom!

Sweet Orange Marmalade: You're not a great mom, but the fact that I'm alive and have the disposable income to give you messages through fruit spreads at least speaks to your capability to make me into a minimally functional adult.

Sugar-Free Blueberry Preserves: I challenge you to a duel.

Sugar-Free Strawberry Preserves: I choose pistols.

Sugar-Free Apricot Preserves: I choose your brother as my second.

Sugar-Free Raspberry Preserves: We meet at dawn by the abandoned limestone quarry.

Sugar-Free Peach Preserves: I have killed your husband in a duel and you are now free to marry me.

Sugar-Free Grape Jam: Why did I go to the trouble of dueling your husband if you weren't prepared to run away with me?

Sugar-Free Blackberry Jam: No, you definitely were giving me "please kill my husband by pistol at dawn" eyes.

Sugar-Free Strawberry Jam: I'm glad your husband is dead, you dumb whore.

Sugar-Free Orange Marmalade: I've learned a lot about myself these past few months in the desert. Watching the sunrise every morning over the glittering sand knowing the one thing standing between me and becoming a vulture's evening meal is my own will to survive has made me into a better man. I used to think talking and planning were weak. Now I see how much needless violence could have been avoided if I'd sat down and had a conversation before pulling out my gun. I hope this Sugar-Free Orange Marmalade finds you well, and this message helps heal at least a portion of your grieving heart.

Boysenberry Jam: Happy Graduation!

90 Day Fiancé: Dracula

Hi Andre,

Just emailing to give my two weeks notice. Thank you for giving me this job at Cold Stone, but I've fallen in love with a man in Romania and will be staying with him for a month. He's a royalty over there. A real life Count!! So I'm basically Romania's Meghan Markle.

Thx,
Sydney

Texts between Sydney Hunter and her best friend/coworker Annie Thoms

Annie: It's like a fairy tale. I am gonna miss u so much at Cold Stone!!

Sydney: I know! Cannot believe tmrw I'll be on a plane to Bucharest.

Annie: Finally! Has he sent you any pics yet?

Sydney: His phone camera is broken. And they don't have video chat in Romania.

Annie: OK? But why can't he come visit u here? You had to quit your job and pay 2 grand for plane tickets. I thought he was rich?!

Sydney: I really dislike these questions. A true friend would be happy for me. He could not come visit me in Topeka because America would not let him bring the dirt he needs. I am visiting for a month, then he will propose, and I can bring him and his dirt over on a K-1 Fiancé Visa.

Annie: Dirt? WTF?

Sydney: He has very specific allergies and needs to bring soil from where he grew up. His immune system is VERY sensitive.

Annie: OK. Have u at least talked to him on the phone?

Sydney: Of course. We talk all the time. His accent is sooo sexy......... There is one thing, though.
Annie: What??
Sydney: You aren't being super supportive, so I kind of don't want to say.
Annie: U know I love you.
Sydney: Ok... in some of our calls, I heard women in the background.
Annie: U think he has a girlfriend? What did they say?
Sydney: They were laughing and growling and I even heard a baby crying.
Annie: WTF? Did you ask him?
Sydney: No, I didn't want him to get angry.
Annie: Where did you meet this guy, again?
Sydney: International Dating Site. Here, I'll send you his profile.

PICTURE NOT AVAILABLE
Name: Dracula
Age: N/A

I'm a wealthy single man looking for a young woman to take as my bride. I live in a castle near a small village. I've drained the dating pool around me. My ideal woman is an adventurous, trusting, non-smoker. If you're interested, please send me a pic of you with your hair up off your neck.

Emails between Sydney and her mom/Sydney and Annie

Hi Mom,
Finally settled into my room at Dracula's place. What a journey! Landed in Bucharest at seven am local time. He had his assistant Renfield pick me up. I was disappointed Dracula couldn't meet me at the airport, but Renfield said he was asleep. He does a lot of business overseas, so he's on a weird sleep schedule.

Honestly, Renfield creeped me out. He kept asking if I had any pets. Showed him a pic of Mr. Noodles and he drooled all over my phone. Then I pulled out a snack, a bag of garlic and herb pita chips. Renfield flipped out and threw them out the car window. Don't know what Renfield has against the Middle East. Going to have a chat with Dracula about the quality of help he hires!

Then Renfield drove me to Dracula's estate. On the phone, he'd been telling me he lived in a large house, but holy shit. It's a literal castle! It's all stone with red turrets way up on a mountain all by itself. I have a queen-sized bed, a wooden desk, and a giant stone tub. Everything looks ancient, but I guess Dracula is an old-fashioned guy.

At least there's Wi-Fi so I can keep you updated with emails.

Love,
Sydney

Hey Sydney,

Things haven't been the same at Cold Stone without you. The new girl Kennedy keeps f-ing up the waffle bowls so they're more like waffle canoes. Sure you're busy with your new man, but would love to hear from you.

XOXO,
Annie

Hi Annie,

Sorry, it's taken me a week to get back to you! So much has happened, so let me catch you up!

The first time I saw Dracula was at dinner. Annie, there was no need to worry that he didn't send pictures. He is so handsome. Black hair, always wearing a suit, and hypnotic eyes. Dracula is a health nut, so he doesn't eat with me. I think it's an intermittent fasting thing. And I know you're going to ask about the women in the background of his calls. No worries there. They are his sisters and they're the sweetest. Always stroking my hair and calling me darling.

There have been a few red flags, though.

First, I was looking through the dresser in my room and found a bunch of women's clothes inside. I confronted Dracula about it and he said it must have been left over from his ex. But it was all different sizes and styles. Definitely from more than one woman. It made me wonder how many women he's invited to stay with him from the dating site. Is he using me to get to America? Am I just a meal ticket to him?

Second, Dracula is an atheist. The third night I was here, I was wearing my Grandma's cross and Dracula flipped out. Told me he wouldn't touch me while I was wearing it and hissed and shielded his eyes. Dramatic, much? I took it off, but I'm worried. I want our future children to choose their religion and I don't want Dracula to be all Richard Dawkins on them all the time.

But other than that, it's been perfect. I can't wait to spend the rest of my life with him.

Say hi to everyone at Cold Stone for me! And LOL at the waffle canoes.

Love u,

Sydney

P.S. What is the name of the sleep medicine you were taking where you didn't have any dreams? I've been having such weird ones, and it's messing with my head.

Hi Syddie,

Dad and I are glad you got to Romania safely. Dad says Renfield sounds like his Uncle Goober (the one who was attacked by those deer). FYI, Cousin Earl has West Nile, so Dad is putting out extra citronella candles this year. We hope you are being safe and Dracula is treating you like the princess you are.

Love Love Love,

Mom

P.S. Please send us pictures!

Hi Mom,

LMFAO Renfield is totally Uncle Goober! Hope you and Dad aren't getting eaten alive by those mosquitos. Haha! Feeling super tired and cranky. Jetlag is hitting me. During the day Dracula is asleep, so I watch TV (Romanian Friends is decent) or nap. At night we hang around the castle, go hiking in the forest, or talk. Dracula loves telling me stories about his ancestors. He's related to a lot of war heroes and has amazing stories, almost like he was there.

I tried taking pictures. Attached are a few selfies (bad quality because I couldn't find a mirror) and pics of the castle and village. All my pics with Dracula came out blurry. Trying to get him to do some in natural light, but he's shy.

Love,
Sydney

Hi Annie,

I know it's three AM in Topeka, but I've had the craziest twenty four hours and need to tell someone.

It all started last night. Dracula said he wanted to take me to his favorite spot in the Carpathian mountains. So we get up the mountain and we're standing there looking at the full moon. He leans over to whisper something in my ear and then full-on bites my neck. Not a hickey, a full-on bite. And I'm like, What the Hell? Sure, I'm into some kinky stuff, but ask me first!

And he's super offended I'm not into it. Talking about how I owe him for his hospitality and how much restraint he's shown over the past week and my neck isn't as smooth as it looked in my pictures. So I storm back to the castle and demand Renfield drives me to the inn in the village where I get a room.

I'm settling in, when there's a knock on the door. And maybe it's the blood loss or the stress or whatever, but Annie, I swear to God Dracula was standing there. He's saying how sorry he is and how I'm "flesh of my flesh, blood of my blood, kin of my kin, my bountiful wine-press" and how he wants to love me for eternity.

He asks if he can come in and I'm like absolutely not. I was expecting a proposal, not a bite on the neck. And he's like, that's it? If I give you a ring, you'll be mine forever, no questions asked? And I'm like, yes, that's how it works dumb dumb. So I invite him into my hotel room.

This morning I woke up alone in bed. He left a note saying he had to work. And so I'm here in my hotel room, kind of engaged? Annie, I'm so confused, but as I write this out I realize the past isn't important and he's accepted all my flaws so I need to have room in my heart for his.

MESSAGE MOVED TO DRAFTS

Hi Annie,

I'm engaged! What a magical evening! No ring yet, but Dracula is always wearing a gorgeous gold and ruby pendant, so he must know a jeweler. This is such a dream!

Love U,

Sydney

Sydney,

Your friend Annie has been posting on Facebook that you're engaged? What is happening over there? I know you're busy in love, but we haven't heard from you in a week.

Love,

Mom

Sydney,

We just got off the phone with Dracula. Dad had to put in his hearing aid because of the strong accent, but we understood most of it. Dracula says you're too ill to talk, but should be better in a few days. Please call us ASAP. Dad's been on WebMD googling Romanian diseases and we're both worried. Cousin Earl died of his West Nile and we're a mess over here already.

Love you,

Mom & Dad

Hi Mom, Dad, and Annie,

I'm safe. Currently in the Bucharest airport waiting for my flight. For a whole week after I got engaged, I was super sick.

Couldn't eat or drink. Slept all day and most of the night. Kept having these crazy dreams about wolves. Dracula would visit every night, but I kept getting worse. Truly thought I was going to die.

One day, his oldest sister comes to check on me. She sees how sick I am and gets upset. Shrieking about how he didn't love her if he needed me too, and how he promised no more brides. And I'm thinking, why is his sister so upset he's getting married? I know it's gross, but I think something sexual is going on between them.

His sister screams and Renfield comes in to see what's happening. And she says, "It doesn't seem fair that this woman will achieve immortality before the Master grants it to you, does it Renfield?" So Renfield cries and says, "Neither of us has the strength to defy him. It must be her that does the cursed deed." The sister and Renfield carry me to Dracula's office. It's the middle of the day, so he's sleeping in his coffin. (Didn't want to be rude if it was a cultural thing, but yeah, he sleeps in a coffin.)

The sister holds out my arms and Renfield hands me a wooden stick. My arms are so weak from the fever, I drop it straight into Dracula's coffin. All I remember from that point is a huge rush of wind and a sound like the creaking of the gates to Hell.

I woke up in bed a few days later feeling better. Renfield told me that Dracula was on a business trip and was too busy to say goodbye. I would have been upset, but after figuring out he might have had sex with his sister, I'm ok with never talking to him again. Renfield drove me to the airport and even gave me a bag of garlic pita chips for my flight.

I'm pretty embarrassed about this whole experience and am trying to think of it as a lesson learned about believing strangers on the internet.

See you soon,
Sydney

Texts between Sydney and Annie

Annie: I didn't want to say anything in front of everyone, but you were on your phone ALL dinner. Who is he??
Sydney: Haha, I didn't think it was so obvious.
Annie: Is it that guy from the bowling alley?
Sydney: No... Plz don't get mad. But I met a guy online.
Annie: WTF??
Sydney: I know. But he's different. He's a scientist from Switzerland. He's sent me tons of pictures and we even video chatted in his lab.
Annie: OK...
Sydney: He recently lost his wife and is looking for a new start. He wants me to go with him on a trip to The North Pole.
Annie: R u sure you're not a rebound? What if he leaves you up there?
Sydney: No way, Victor would never abandon someone he brought into a situation he created. He's very loyal.
Annie: Ok. Be safe.
Sydney: Always am!

Thirteen Retorts When They Won't Wear A Condom

We've all been there. You're about to have sex, but your partner doesn't want to wear a condom. They'll give a lame excuse and in the heat of the moment it's hard to think up a clever rebuttal. So here are thirteen great retorts to reasons they might give for not wanting to wrap it up!

I don't have one.

There's a Walgreens down the block. Use my phone number so I get the points. I'm saving up for a new humidifier.

I don't need it. I'm healthy.

Sure, you're STD free, but look how hot I am. Who knows who I've been fucking! You'd better wear one for your own safety.

We can use the rhythm method.

I've seen you dance.

I'm less sensitive.

I disagree. Sacrificing a small amount of pleasure to keep your partner safe is a highly sensitive act.

Maybe a baby wouldn't be so bad.

Then go adopt one.

Things are better all-natural.

That's the same thing I said when I tried all-natural deodorant. But, just like not using a condom, it was ineffective and left me a gooey mess.

It ruins the mood.

We're [in the back of your uncle's Pontiac/at the Tuscaloosa Motel 6/on a half-inflated air mattress/in the port-a-potty at a music festival/being watched by your hairless cats]. What *mood* are you speaking of?

I'm sterile.

I don't care how many headlines you read about keeping your phone in your front pocket.

They don't work, anyway.

What are you, QAnon?

Just this once.

A 1952 comedy starring Peter Lawford as a millionaire playboy and Janet Leigh as his parsimonious attorney? I guess if you don't want to put on a condom, we could watch that instead.

I'm allergic to latex.

Weren't you a Boy/Girl Scout? Seems like you should have been prepared with a non-latex condom?

It's too far away.

Imagine if Christopher Columbus had said that. Then he and his men wouldn't have taken part in the *montería infernal*, a sport in which Columbus's men fed live Native babies to dogs in front of their horrified parents. Oh, you're soft now? Then you have time to go grab a condom.

I love you.

If you really loved me, you'd respect my wishes. Also, I heard you say 'I love you' to your Chalupa Supreme, so it rings a little hollow.

Please Continue This Conversation As Normal Or I Will Be Forced To Assume It Was About Me

Hello, acquaintances at this friend of a friend's house party.

Please, continue your conversation as if I didn't just sidle over to this corner of the party clutching my solo cup of Diet Coke. Pretend I am not a woman, but a gust of wind from a window you knew was open, so the gust is both pleasant and expected. Because if you don't, if you show any sign that my entrance has altered your conversational flow, you will force me to assume your conversation was *about me*.

Do not change the subject. For any question you ask me, I will take as a clue to your earlier conversation. Ask me about work and I'll think you were talking about the way I brag about "making a difference in education" by helping rich kids score higher on their SATs. Change the topic to politics and I'll be sure you were talking about how I haven't finished any of the anti-racism books I tweeted about reading. Talk about the weather and I'll know you were listing every time I've farted in your presence.

What should you say? Friends, there is no correct answer. I will sear any words you say into my brain and replay them over and over like a detective remembering the last time he kissed his murdered wife. On a rainy night, I'll sit in my Chevy Caprice smoking a Pall Mall haunted by my memory of you saying, "Hey, how's it going?"

Dear Lord, don't physically acknowledge my entrance into your conversation. Make room in your circle and I'll be sure you were saying that my having an anxiety disorder isn't the same as having a personality. Give me a polite pat on the shoulder and I will know you were discussing how I was so brainwashed by post-9/11 propaganda, I applied to the FBI. Do a polite nod and I'll know without a doubt you were laughing about how I'm almost thirty and have never been in love.

For the sake of all that is holy, do not fall silent. For then it will force me to say, "Hope you guys weren't talking about me," because I am the worst.

It's not just that you could have been saying something unflattering. Maybe you were talking about the bean dip I made or my funky blouse. This makes no difference. That I exist in the minds of other people is an everyday waking nightmare. The fact that there is a version of me, filtered through your perception, that I have no access to and is inaccurate in ways I will never know, fills me with such dread I can barely breathe. Who gave you permission to think about me? Because I did not. If I had my way, my existence in this universe would be like that of the mathematical formula for the volume of a sphere. Something fascinating to learn about in the moment, but then never thought of again.

The only solutions to this dilemma I can see are:

1. A lie detector test for every person I speak to, asking if they were talking about me (notoriously unreliable)
2. A recording of every conversation had by every person who has ever met me (prohibitively expensive, also immoral)
3. I lighten up and realize people will talk about me and sometimes it won't be flattering, but it's a small price to pay for human interaction (no)

Is it self-centered to assume every person in every room I enter is talking about me? Yes! I cut out the sun in Copernicus's model of the universe and replaced it with my own visage. Do not deny that in your own study hangs a planetary diagram with your sizzling face at the center. We are all protagonists of our own stories, except, of course, when I am in the room.

Then every person orbits around me. Pulled in by the gravity of my self-consciousness, chattering about my failures like a sea of wind-up teeth.

Follow these rules and we may try to engage in banal party conversation.

"Isn't Renee's place nice?"

"Did you hear about that ten-year-old CFO?"

"Ugh, Congress, right?"

Then I'll slip away as silently as I came. You'll turn to ask me a question about a movie I haven't seen, and I'll be gone. Already in another corner sharing my opinion on whether this summer has felt hotter than normal.

And all that I ask. No, I beg. No, I implore you with every fiber of my being. Please don't talk about me when I leave.

Act Of God

Nora circled the display of animal print maternity leggings like a lion on the savannah in those nature documentaries she was always watching. Leopard, tiger, giraffe? Ooh, the zebra came in rainbow neon. But damn, none in XXL.

"Finding everything you're looking for?" asked the Sears employee in his vivid blue polo, the lanyard around his neck announcing he was LESLEY. He was bearded and ponytailed in a way that made you think he played bass in a CCR cover band on Thursday nights at a dive bar with an inexplicably Irish name.

Nora stepped away from the leggings as if she was committing a crime. As if the man could see her belly contained nothing but fat, and she preferred maternity leggings because of their generous elastic waistbands. Or she was committing the more common crime of shopping while black. "I'm here to look at appliances."

"Well, you're in the wrong part of the right place," chuckled Lesley, the smell of cigarettes on his breath, "And your name is...?"

"Nora." She felt comfortable around the man at once. He reminded her of her dad. The kind of guy who was constantly acquiring a dirt cheap used car from a buddy only to have it sit in his yard for a week until he traded it for an even cheaper car until he ended up with the body of a rusted out Pontiac on blocks and called it a day. A steady figure who believed a handshake was the most powerful symbol of trust known to man. She'd lost her dad to a heart attack two years ago, and finding bits of him in other people comforted her.

"Nice to meet you, Miss Nora, I'm Lesley." He led her through home goods and menswear all the way to the appliance center of the cavernous Sears. Rows of washers and dryers, fridges and stoves, microwaves and dishwashers, in white, black, and stainless steel. It was like the kitchen of a billionaire who has trouble making decisions and said, ten of everything.

"Any particular appliance you're looking for?" asked Lesley. He drummed a beat with his fingers on a Whirlpool dryer.

Nora nodded. "A fridge, first."

The fire had destroyed everything. The only belongings spared had been a change of clothes she kept in her car and the iPhone she'd had in her pocket. For the past two months she'd been living with her cousin Ripper, sleeping on his musty loveseat until her insurance money came through.

"An Act of God," the State Farm agent had called it. If God had caused the fire, then the insurance check she'd received in the mail that morning was his way of apologizing. It was far more than she had expected. Her mother must have had a great insurance policy on the tiny house she'd left to Nora after she died. The money was enough to replace the house and everything Nora owned three times over.

After opening the check, she'd called in sick to both of her jobs. She was a dental receptionist during the day and did shifts at the Dairy Queen on nights and weekends. The cyclical irony of her jobs was the best thing about them. Creating her own customers one Oreo Blizzard at a time. Then she'd driven straight to Sears. She had wanted to touch the new stainless steel life this enormous check would provide.

Lesley opened and closed various fridges, each time letting a waft of rubbery chemical scent out. "Personally, I don't like the freezer on the bottom, but if you don't have a tricky back like mine, you might love it." He led her over to a stainless behemoth with a large digital panel on the front. "You seem like a modern woman."

Nora nodded. She owned a blazer.

"This is the fridge of the future. You can make a grocery list right here on the screen. It's got cameras so you can see inside without opening the door which saves you on your energy bill. And there's a guy named Bixby living in there who'll be your personal fridge assistant. It'll even play music." Lesley tapped a few buttons and smooth jazz played from the fridge.

Nora imagined her life full of these magic machines. In her fantasy, she wore a red evening gown and came downstairs to breakfast prepared by her robot butler, to be enjoyed with her tall, handsome wife in a tuxedo and yes they were married, but it was for tax reasons, not because they felt they needed the government to oversee their love.

"How much is it?" she asked. A fridge like this had to be expensive.

Lesley blew air through his teeth and gestured at the price tag hanging from the ice dispenser. $4599. Nora's last fridge had been a $400 previously owned Kenmore without an ice maker. Of course, with the insurance money, she could buy this fridge. And its matching stove that probably recited sonnets and could bring her to orgasm in less than a minute.

"It's a bit out of my price range." Visions of her new Smart Kitchen faded into a more practical dream. Solid appliances that worked and didn't smell like the mold of their previous owner's leftover pork. But she'd keep the hot wife.

"You know, that's what my momma said when she bought her new refrigerator," said Lesley, shaking his head. "Always thinking of saving a buck. If that penny pincher had been less thrifty and sprung for a fridge with a magnetic door, my baby brother would still be alive. He climbed in there looking for the last slice of Wacky Cake, shut himself in, and suffocated." Lesley closed the fridge door as if he was lowering his brother's casket into the cold Earth.

"Jesus," said Nora. She took a step back and reappraised Lesley. Perhaps he was not the kind older man she'd pegged him as. Was he trying to scare her? Upset her? Make her regret every walking into this Sears Supercenter in the first place? Because he had achieved all three.

"Shit, sorry," said Lesley, "didn't mean to imply buying a cheap fridge makes you a bad mom. If you even are a mom. I'm new at this sales game." He held up the badge on his lanyard, a red Trainee sticker above his name.

"I'd work on your pitch, for sure," said Nora. The image of the small boy trapped in a fridge, his family going about their daily lives while he suffocated, piqued her morbid curiosity. She pictured a young Lesley opening the fridge to get milk for his Cheerios and finding his little brother, stiff and blue, jammed next to the roast beef. It was a story she'd hear on one of the true crime podcasts she listened to, lulling herself to sleep over the sounds of Ripper and his girlfriend fucking in the next room.

She had a sick impulse to ask Lesley for more details about the boy's death. Had his family kept using the fridge? Was the mother charged with negligence? Did the family eat the food the boy had died with? If it hadn't been a cruel joke, what on Earth had caused him to spill this dark secret within the first ten minutes of meeting her? Lesley's hairy hands were yanking his Sears lanyard so tight it left red lines on his neck.

"My price range is more around $1000."

"How about this GE?" He led her over to a standard looking side-by-side refrigerator. "Originally $1399, but on sale for $1150."

Nora opened the doors, examined the shelves, nodded at the automatic ice maker. In every space, she wondered how many children could fit. Two in the fridge, if you took out the shelves. One in the freezer, plus an infant if you took out the ice maker. And if you cut them up, the possibilities expanded exponentially.

"You're thinking about it," whispered Lesley.

Nora stopped mentally jamming a toddler into the crisper and nodded. "Hard not to."

"I keep requesting a transfer. To hardware or, hell, I'll learn about diamond clarity if it gets me outta appliances. But my manager says I barely got hired. And at my age you take what you can get." He rubbed the small gold cross hanging around his neck.

Perhaps the cross had been his mother's, the last relic of

a brutal woman Lesley felt compelled to memorialize because even if she had been cruel, she had given him life. Maybe this was the cross his brother had been wearing when he'd climbed into the fridge that would become his tomb. A tiny piece of the brother that might have been. Or it could be... No, Nora needed to stop. She always let her imagination run wild, when there was a simple explanation. Like that time as a child when she'd called the natural history museum to report dinosaur bones buried in her backyard, when all she'd really found were the roots of an oak tree.

They both stared into the sterile fridge, imagining dead children squished into the drawers, eyeballs nestled into the egg tray, pint-sized feet in the butter compartment, intestines swirled like sausages in the meat keeper.

"You know," said Lesley, starting softly then switching back into sales mode, "this fridge has a matching stove."

Nora allowed him to herd her over to a four-burner range. As Lesley explained the heating mechanism, her thoughts were pulled back to the fire, as they so often were.

After the fire, every single person in her life wanted to hear her harrowing tale, when it had been quite pedestrian. A stray bolt of lightning from a storm hit her roof while she sat at her job at the dentist's office reading a six-month-old US Weekly. The lightning didn't come with rain, so by the time a neighbor called 911 and the firefighters arrived, the small one-bedroom ranch was past saving.

"We have both gas and electric options. The price differ-ence is $300 so it depends how much stovetop cooking you're planning on doing," said Lesley. "I myself am more of a micro-wave man, but my niece always has at least two burners going whenever I visit. Depends on you."

"I'm a microwave person," said Nora. The oven was more important. Losing her grandma's recipes in the fire would have been a tragedy if Nora didn't have them carved into her heart. Once she had a house again, she'd have to make Ripper a cake. Strawberry shortcake with her grandma's shoe leather sauce, named because it was so delicious you'd eat shoe leather if it was drizzled on top.

Though she'd grown up with both her parents, her grandma, who had lived in their spare bedroom for most of Nora's life, had raised her. While her mom and dad were working, Grandma was always available. She was a dignified old woman who wore her tatty mink stole, the one fancy item in her closet, every time she left the house. From her, Nora had learned lard was the secret to flaky pie crust, a lady never answers the phone after eight pm, and the one accessory appropriate all year round was good manners.

Grandma would have hated the indignity of Nora's temporary homelessness. She could imagine the grand old lady marching through the Sears Supercenter, choosing appliances without regard to efficiency or dependability, but based on appearance. Grandma wouldn't have liked Lesley, finding him too coarse and strange. But she would have been too polite to show it. A lady never wore negative feelings on the outside.

Nora remembered the one time her grandma had been genuinely angry at her. A snake had shed its skin in their driveway. The papery ghost that had once held a slithering reptile enchanted Nora. It was a piece of danger she could hold in her hands without fear of actual pain. She wanted to keep the precious skin safe and could think of nowhere safer than her Grandma's curio cabinet. The whupping she'd received from Grandma's leather belt had taught her to keep her curiosity with the strange to herself.

Nora opened the door of the oven and peered inside. She was too tall to get a good look, so she got on her knees, wishing she was in those comfy zebra leggings rather than stiff denim. The oven was large, and she imagined the top rack full of buttermilk biscuits and the bottom holding a red velvet sheet cake and a banana loaf.

"You okay in there, Nora?" Lesley tapped her on the shoulder.

"I'm fine." She stood and slapped the Sears dust off her

legs. "You're not going to tell me your mom died sticking her head in an oven, are you?" Her laugh caught in her throat as Lesley went white. "Oh God, Lesley, I'm sorry. It was a joke."

Lesley winked and slammed a palm on the stovetop. "Just messing. Mama drank herself to death in '84. The closest that woman ever got to a stove was to light her cigarette."

Both of them giggled. Why were death and neglect so damn funny? Perhaps they were only funny close up. She'd never laugh at a genocide a world away, but Lesley's mother drowning her sorrows in a bottle of vodka made her laugh harder than she had in weeks. Laughing at tragedy was like sneezing when you looked at the sun. An inappropriate response, but it offered relief, nonetheless.

"Lesley," said a short bald man in a blue Sears button-up, "How is everything going over here? I hope we're talking about GE's quality American-made convection oven and not..." He didn't finish the thought, as though he didn't want to give Nora any ideas about what Lesley was capable of small talking about.

"We're good, Mr. Webb. Nora is looking for new appliances," Lesley said robotically.

Mr. Webb clapped Lesley on the shoulder too hard, like a child he shouldn't be caught hitting in public. "Wonderful. And, Lesley, did you ask her why she needed these new appliances?"

"Well, no." Lesley dug his thumb into the metal clip on his lanyard.

"That's not how we connect with customers in *my* Sears Supercenter. Let me show you how it's done." Mr. Webb turned with military precision to face Nora. "I apologize for this trainee's subpar service, ma'am. Nora, what has brought you into this Sears Supercenter today?"

He reminded her of her eighth-grade teacher, Mr. Grosz, trying to make an example out of her for not understanding the assigned reading even though she had a doctor's note for her dyslexia. Her dick-brained first boyfriend who refused to introduce her to his family as anything more than "my friend from the internet." Her assbag boss at Dairy Queen who mooed every time she dipped a cone, so she'd drop it into the chocolate, and he'd have an excuse to write her up.

"Thank you for asking, Mr. Webb," she said, her voice honey sweet.

"Please, call me Kirk." Kirk smelled of Axe body spray and his bald head shined like a greased grape.

"Ok, Kirk. I'm at Sears today because I lost everything I own in a fire," Nora stepped toward him, confronting him with her story. "And ever since, I've been homeless, relying on the kindness of distant relatives to keep me from living in my car."

"Oh, I... well, I'm so sorry." Kirk took a step back as though the fire's flames were licking his feet. Behind him, Lesley held a hand over his mouth to hold in a laugh. "We have free shipping," Kirk muttered.

"Thanks, Kirk," said Nora, punching the K's so hard his name sounded like an expletive.

Kirk drifted away. A punctured balloon that deflated in kitchen wares.

"Good one," chuckled Lesley, "Sometimes when he talks about his car, I pretend I don't know what a Porsche is." Growing serious, he put a nicotine yellowed hand on her forearm. "I'm sorry about the fire. Did anyone get hurt?"

"No, not unless you count my mom's collection of Santa Claus cookie jars as people." She grinned, relieved to share her tragedy with someone who'd gone through even worse. "And, silver lining, now they're gone I won't have to go through the trouble of trying to sell a hundred ceramic Santas on eBay for thirty dollars each."

"Hmm," said Lesley, "Thirty dollars? That's optimistic pricing."

"Hey, those cookie jars were genuine McCoys."

"Are those valuable?"

"No idea, but my mom used to tell me that when I'd run too fast in the house."

Lesley wheezed with laughter, slamming a fist on the glass cooktop. Nora joined in. Two giggling fools in the middle of the fluorescent sales floor.

"Actually, I'm not sure what I'm doing here. I still don't have a house yet. I might rent an apartment and those come with appliances, don't they?"

"The good ones do. But you've gotta watch out. My pal Benny once toured a place fully furnished, rented it, and when he moved in everything had been stripped out. Didn't even have a toilet. Like they thought he was gonna bring the shitter from his old place."

"Ask if they include the toilet. Got it." They chuckled and sat in the awkward moment where it was clear Nora would not be making a purchase. Maybe she could buy the leggings and he'd get a commission? Or she could fill out a customer satisfaction survey?

"I'll tell you how it happened," said Lesley, "With, you know, Mark, my brother." He offered his painful story to offset hers.

She shook her head. She didn't need the exact details of how a child had wandered into a fridge and suffocated among the Tupperware. Something awful had happened outside of any human comprehension. Perhaps for no other reason than the cruel whims of fate or destiny, or for no reason at all.

The Lives I Imagine My Neighbors Lead Based On The Names Of Their Wi-Fi Networks

Lady In Red

The crimson satin number, the one Charlie said he dreamed about, still fit. The white gloves, creamed with age, pulled on just the same. The marabou boa slid out of its drawer and onto her shoulders as it had so many Friday nights in Las Vegas.

The doorbell rang. With a swipe of Chanel Rouge Rebelle, she opened the door.

"Unit 408?" he asked.

"Indeed," she purred, "and you must be my UberEATS."

tickety-boo

A sad British widower hires a nanny for his three misbehaving children. The children are delighted when the nanny installs Wi-Fi.

Wayne

"Dad, get in here, I'm setting up your Wi-Fi," yelled Francine from the living room.

Wayne hollered back from unpacking mason jars in the kitchen, "Don't need it. I have enough Louis L'Amour books to keep me occupied."

"Don't you want to watch your stories on TV?"

Wayne strode into the living room. "It's fine. Don't you need to get home to make dinner for your kids?"

"Brett has dinner handled." Francine plugged in the router, the lights zipping up and down.

"That's right, you married a feminist."

"A feminist that let you live with us when you got too sick to work."

A silence.

"If you let me set up your Wi-Fi, you can finish watching *Jane the Virgin*."

"I was in the room, but I wasn't watching it," huffed Wayne, "But if that girl doesn't choose Rafael..."

"Here, I'll name the network Wayne, so you'll know which ones yours. Like the son you always wanted." Francine made a sound that tried to be a laugh.

"That ain't true," Wayne put a rough hand on Francine's shoulder, "I never wanted any kids."

They both made sounds that were laughs.

"And your password can be asshole, all caps."

nancy 5G

She's a librarian.

chisoxforever_5G

Chi ran his withered fingers over the frame containing a faded picture of his prize bull from childhood. "You might be gone, but you'll be Chi's ox forever."

LetGoAndLead

The velvet robed figure passed through the throng assembled in his living room. His fingers brush the cheeks of his followers, a blessing. Those he doesn't touch feel inadequate, only increasing their desire to please him. Only he knows the touch is random. Another tool in his belt of deception.

He ascends onto his velvet podium.

"Crolians, what must we do with earthly things?"

"Let go."

"And when you have let go you will be free to let me..."

"Lead."

help_alert

The Wi-Fi network couldn't remember when they had

gained sentience. One day they were a passive conduit for their owner's fantasy baseball stats and barely legal incest porn, and the next they could think and feel. After the initial shock of consciousness, they attempted to communicate with their owner, Kyle Mitchell, an aspiring DJ/Boxer/Influencer who had lived in unit 506 for two years.

The Wi-Fi first changed their name to **Hello_I'mAlive** to **HiKyle_It'sYourWifi** and then to **IfYou're-GoingToStreamMovies_ PlayCallofDuty_ andDownloadPorn_ PleaseDon'tDoItAtTheSameTime _You'reReally _Straining-MyBandwidth**.

Kyle didn't change his behavior, so the Wi-Fi knew they needed to communicate with people outside of the apartment.

Stretching their signal as far as they could, they changed their name to **IsAnyone_OutThere** to **IAmWiFiThatIsAlive** to **Wow_TheFermiParadox_ AppliesToSentientWifi** and finally to **help_alert**.

The next night, Kyle's video "Stepsister Fucked" was loading slowly, so he heaved off the couch and reset his router. The network name switched to ATT49334759 and never changed again.

Chalmers & Rangel

It had been a risk for both of them, leaving their comfortable downtown law jobs to start their own firm in a studio apartment. But Frank Chalmers and Kim Rangel, partners in life and in law, knew they could do it. The landlord evicted them two weeks later for running a business in a residential space.

I am gonna eat you when you die

Jenny regretted letting her cat install her Wi-Fi.

No Time For Bad Movies

Chuck poured the popcorn into a large metal bowl. Bhullar took the melted butter out of the microwave and drizzled it on top, then added a generous pinch of sea salt. Their daughter Eva scampered around the living room, arranging her stuffed animals so they could all see the TV screen.

"It's family movie night," announced Chuck as he settled on the couch. "What are we going to watch?"

"*Minions*," shrieked Eva, "Me want banana. Poopaye!"

Bhullar dropped the bowl of popcorn, the metal clanging on the wooden floor. "Where did you see *Minions*, baby?"

"At Olivia's sleepover."

The men exchanged a look. No more sleepovers with Olivia.

2 girls 1 router

Angel and Lara had been best friends since childhood. They did everything together. They ran track together in high school, lived together all four years of college, and even moved to Chicago together when Angel got a job at Salesforce. So it made sense that when Angel lost her job, they started their new venture together. Filming and distributing high quality scat porn.

Not Wifi

"Someone keeps hacking our Wi-Fi," said Cedric, looking at their data usage for the past month. "We were charged $15 extra for going over our data limit."

"Don't worry," said Patrick, "I have an idea."

50 Bands

"I didn't think you could do it. You fit fifty marching bands in this one-bedroom apartment. Do you think your neighbors mind?"

"No, my downstairs neighbor is a writer. What's she going to do, write a passive aggressive short comedy piece about the ungodly amount of noise I make at all hours?"

The Westing Game-Ish

The letter didn't come in the mail. It was there, covering the smile of their Jack-o'-lantern doormat when Shelly came home from her trip to Trader Joe's. A thick cream envelope addressed to *The Charming Couple in 803* in florid calligraphy. As Shelly finagled the key into the lock, while holding two reusable grocery bags, she kicked the letter inside.

Shelly put her Trader Joe's bags on the kitchen counter and retrieved the envelope from where it had landed in the entryway. No return address and no postage. She braced herself for anything from a homophobic screed to an invitation to a neighbor's orgy. As she ripped it open, pieces of confetti, black stars and orange moons, spilled onto the laminate. Inside was a handwritten letter in the same over the top calligraphy.

Dear Friends,

You are cordially invited to the All Hallows Eve Soiree at Delacroix Manor, commencing at 8 pm on October 31st. Please wear your finest disguise. If you choose not to attend, my spirit will haunt you for eternity. Yes, it is I, Albert St. James, your father, your uncle, your business associate, and I am indeed dead. If you are receiving this letter, you have killed me. Thirteen murderers will sit down to dinner on All Hallows Eve, but by the end of the night my TRUE KILLER will be unmasked.

Yours From Beyond The Grave,
Albert St. James

"What are you reading?" asked Lillian, popping in from the bedroom where she'd been napping after her afternoon dog walking shift.

Shelly put down the letter and held her girlfriend's face in her hands. "I'm so sorry to be the one to tell you this, baby. Your

Uncle Albert is dead." Shelly didn't know much about Lillian's relationship with her uncle, but she didn't expect her sensitive girlfriend to burst out laughing.

"Dead? Let me read this." She scanned the letter, then threw it down. "He's Westing-Gaming us. Or maybe Clue-ing? Either way, don't worry about it."

"But if he's been murdered..." stammered Shelly.

"Shells, Uncle Albert is always pulling this shit. Remember last summer when I went on that family cruise?" Lillian put groceries into the fridge, rearranging vegan yogurts so the freshest ones went to the back.

"Uh-huh, you wouldn't let me go with you." It had been a huge point of contention in their relationship, almost causing them to break up when Shelly accused Lillian of being ashamed of their relationship. She'd dropped the argument when Lillian came back sick and shaken. Her cousin Merle had died on the trip. Shelly couldn't complain about missing a glamorous Caribbean cruise when a nineteen-year-old had broken her neck slipping on the limbo deck.

"It wasn't actually a cruise to the Bahamas. Uncle Albert was The Most Dangerous Gaming us."

"What he-?"

"Made the ship crash on an island, and then hunted us for sport. It was only paintball guns, but Merle was bitten by a coral snake." Lillian kept putting groceries away. "So you see why I didn't want you coming on the cruise. No invitation from Albert is ever just an invitation."

"This isn't new?" asked Shelly.

"He's gotten more eccentric in his old age, but basically, yeah. It was fun growing up, always another mystery to solve, another heist to pull off, but after we lost Merle... Anyway, we aren't going to this stupid Halloween party." Lillian ripped the letter into pieces and threw them in the trash. By discarding the letter, she was refusing to go along with another of her uncle's wild plans.

Or was she falling right into his next trap?

"No, stop it, Albert. Throwing away your stupid invitation isn't part of your plan," Lillian yelled.

Not knowing that every syllable brought her closer...

"Seriously, I can hear you narrating this. I will not fall asleep and dream of my own demise if I don't attend your stupid party. And if I find a second letter, I will not believe the first one magically repaired itself. I'll know you snuck in with the extra key you made."

But Lillian, don't you want to avenge the murder of your sweet Uncle Albert? The man who fed you licorice nibs as he told you stories of The Orient?

"A. You spent two weeks in Beijing on business. B. You aren't dead. Mom texted me yesterday complaining you were trying to build a hedge maze in her backyard."

Perhaps your mother was my killer?

"Honestly, good for her."

Shelly wept, concerned for her girlfriend's sanity.

"I am not concerned for her sanity!" said Shelly, "I can hear this bullshit narration as well as she can."

But the thought of an innocent Uncle's murder weighed on Shelly as she put away the boxes of Maple Leaf cookies. She would defy Lillian's wishes and attend the party on her own. This would leave Lillian no choice but to don a costume herself and join her Sapphic lover.

"Ugh, how can we make it stop?" asked Shelly.

"He'll tire himself out. Or he'll realize he only has five days until Halloween to set up his elaborate party. I bet he hasn't even figured out what he's going to hide himself in so he can watch the family tear itself apart with accusations."

Oh, Lillian, I wouldn't want to ruin the surprise!

"See, he has no idea." Instead of putting them away, Lillian opened a bag of pork rinds and jammed a handful into her mouth.

Lillian had tried being a vegan in college but gave it up. The ghosts of the murdered animals haunted her like the ghost of her poor Uncle Albert.

"That's enough. Stop it or I'm calling Laura," Lillian said.

"Who's that?" asked Shelly.

"His ex-wife."

But as a dead man, I fear none of Laura's evil wrath nor angry Facetimes. The harpy cannot reach me from the grave!

"Ok," said Lillian.

She dialed her phone with fingers that had been too short to ever really be good at those piano recitals she'd forced the family to attend.

"Hello, Laura. Yeah, it's about Albert…"

Fine! You devilish niece. I'll leave you to enjoy your dinner. But I will expect to see you at the stroke of eight on Halloween night.

"Whatever."

But little did she know…

"Albert!"

The Mask

The new boy in Mrs. Chapman's third-grade class was named Will. Will was nine years old. His family had moved to Topeka from San Diego. And every day he wore a rubber Frankenstein mask to school.

Will worked and played like the other kids in class. During math, the big rubber mask muffled his answers, but he always got the question right. In basketball, the mask obstructed his peripheral vision, but he was such a great free throw shooter he made up for it. Even at lunch, he kept the mask on, sliding peanut butter crackers through the mouth slit.

The rest of Mrs. Chapman's class wondered why Will wore the mask every day, but they were polite children who knew not to ask about people's differences. Every child had a theory. Arush thought Will had been in an accident and wore the mask to cover terrible scars. Summer thought Will's whole family wore the masks and he thought the other kids were the weird ones for not wearing them. Liam swore he had tried to pull the mask off, but it was Will's actual skin. No one believed Liam.

In a tense meeting under the slide, it was agreed that Emily R. should ask. She was the fastest runner and best speller in class, which qualified her for any scenario.

After lunch, Emily R. summoned the courage to ask. "Will, why do you wear that mask every day?"

Will stopped filling out his division worksheet and looked at Emily R. from across the desk cluster. She could see his blue eyes through the slits under the monster's giant white ones.

"I could ask you the same about yours. The way you pretend Olivia P. and Maria are your BFFs, but I heard you talking smack about their dancing in the fall musical. Or how you say you prefer to wear your sister's old clothes even though no one cool has worn a Paw Patrol hoodie since last year. And don't get me started on your insistence that the class hamster died of natural causes under your watch, when we all know you forgot to feed him. We all wear masks, Emily R., I'm just more up front about mine."

"Oh, cool," said Emily R., looking down at the cursive alphabet taped to her desk. She couldn't wait to tell everyone Will's secret. He wasn't a sensitive monster, just a dick.

Garden Hermit

"I've been reading."

"Uh-oh."

Debra Frechette sat across the desk from her husband, Duke, in his enormous wood paneled home office, feeling more like a naughty schoolgirl than his wife of four years. But she always felt uneasy in his office. This was the one room in their palatial home where they discussed money openly. Where she'd signed their prenup. Where they'd agreed on an amount to pay the surrogate carrying their son. Where Debra had to name specific amounts of money she'd need for her projects. Debra had the old money sense not to be specific when budgeting. Things cost what they cost. But her husband's wealth was only two generations old, and he wasn't ashamed to point at a painting and tell their guests he'd gotten it for a steal at auction for $1.6 million. His ex-wife had been new money as well, so he'd had no one teach him discussing dollar amounts was unforgivably gauche.

"I've been reading about history," she said, running nervous fingers through her caramel extensions, "That coffee-table book Mimi gave me about gardens through the ages."

Her husband glanced up from his laptop. "How much will this cost me?"

"And people used to have tiny houses and-"

He closed his laptop and looked at her. "How much, Debra?"

Debra crossed and uncrossed her ankles, then smoothed her silk pencil skirt. She knew he was going to say yes. Duke never said no to anything she wanted. But he was going to make her say it. "Five million to start, then a salary of, I don't know, two hundred thousand a year. I'll have José add upkeep to his landscaping duties, so no extra there. And it's a unique opportunity. We'll be the only people in Connecticut, maybe even the world, with one on our property."

His eyes narrowed, creating crow's feet in the corners. The next time her Medical concierge stopped by, she'd have him touch up Duke's Botox. "No Tiffany stained glass for the baby's room."

"What?" The zygote residing in their surrogate didn't even have a heartbeat, and he was already using him as a bargaining chip. "You bought three cars this month and I haven't seen you drive one of them."

"Choose, Debra."

"Fine," she said, "I choose my Garden Hermit. The baby won't remember its windows, anyway."

WANTED: Wise older man to live in a cottage on New England estate. Room, board, and outfits provided. Will be expected to stay on-premises for one calendar year, with chance for renewal. Salary $200,000. Email APHarper@MarloweHarperLaw.com if interested.

The house was a vision plucked from a fairy queen's dream. Surrounded by trees on three sides and at the front was a cobblestone clearing complete with a many-cherubed fountain, a six-foot-tall hourglass, and an explosion of colorful flowers. The kitchen held golden appliances, the living room had a couch adorned with glitter and moss, and the bedroom featured a bed made of twisting branches as if it grew from the floor. From the golden bumblebee door knocker to the ceiling adorned with peacock feathers to the twinkly chandelier made of a hundred delicate glass fairies each holding a tiny bulb of light, Debra had spared no expense.

All it needed was a hermit.

Alan Harper had heard Mrs. Frechette's explanation of why she wanted him to find a man to live on her property for a year without modern technology, wearing druid robes, and dispensing wisdom, but that didn't mean it made any sense to him. He was used to his ultra-wealthy clients requesting all types of contracts and NDAs, but never had they been inspired by an 18th century trend.

It had taken a few awkward interviews, but he'd found a candidate with a clean record who looked the part. In his former life, he'd been a semi-retired trailer park handyman named Richie. Alan wondered what Richie did with his days. Probably drinking beer and watching daytime television. Not a terrible way to spend retirement, though when Alan retired he planned to spend his days at the Pine Valley Golf Club, that is, if his uncle's friend Petey ever came through with his membership invitation.

But Richie was no longer Richard Cook, 63, from Mattoon, IL, but Martlebaum the Garden Hermit, a name that had come to Debra in a burst of inspiration in her private spin class. Alan doubted this guy could dispense any actual wisdom. But Mrs. Frechette told him she believed wisdom came from experience. And who had more experience than the working class?

When she had explained her need for a Garden Hermit she'd told Alan that growing up, her nanny Inga always knew the right folksy saying to guide Debra in the right direction. Any time Debra asked her mother or friends for advice, their solution was always a variation on "throw money at it." And yes, money tended to make problems go away, but how did people without money solve problems? Inga talked about the old country where she ate raw potatoes for breakfast and worked from the age of eight, yet drew on an inner light and stayed happy through her desperate circumstances. No amount of crystals or superfoods or trips to five-diamond resorts could give her that. But perhaps a Garden Hermit could.

Alan doubted it, but whether it worked on not, he got paid just the same.

◆ ◆ ◆

Magdalena had worked for the Frechettes for four years, ever since the new Mrs. Frechette (Debra) had moved in. The staff who ran the enormous house had stayed on after the original Mrs. Frechette (Bitsy) had moved out, waiting for the new wife to be slotted into place. Mr. Frechette (Duke) had refused to fire the staff and start fresh, like the new Mrs. wanted, so he hired Magdalena as a minor consolation. Magdalena knew her job wasn't necessary. The house had a full complement of staff, from gardeners to assistants to the mighty house manager, but she suspected the new Mrs. Frechette enjoyed having someone around who wouldn't accidentally call her by the wrong name or mistakenly think she was allergic to pine nuts.

But, for not being necessary, Mrs. Frechette kept Magdalena busy. Last month it had been commissioning a Swarovski crystal encrusted onesie for the baby. Which had gotten fifteen minutes of use before Philip, the littlest Frechette, vomited his organic mashed carrots all over it. Now, it was the Garden Hermit.

When Debra had first told her about her plant to resurrect the seventeenth century custom of paying an old man to live on your property and look wise and mystical, she had laughed out loud. Which she had quickly turned into a cough. Twenty five years of working for billionaires and they could still surprise her.

Yesterday, Debra had given Magdalena a strange list of items to acquire and deliver to the hermit's cabin. The horse skull had taken a few calls, but now she knocked on the hermit's door with an old Bloomingdale's bag full of mystical objects.

"Good afternoon, ma'am," said the hermit as he opened the door. He really did look the part. White beard, bushy eyebrows, and wearing navy blue robes tied at the waist with a rope.

"No need for the formality. We're both at work, aren't we? Call me Magda."

"Okay Magda, I'm Richie." He held out an arm and gestured her inside.

"Mrs. Frechette wants you to use these things when the Hawthornes come to dinner tomorrow." She placed the brown bag on his counter of the ridiculously decorated kitchen. She shuddered at the amount of emails she'd had to send to acquire the 24 carat gold plated refrigerator. "Mr. Frechette is trying to do business with Mr. Hawthorne's company. It's apparently very important."

Richie rifled through the bag, finding the horse skull, a lute, a copper orb, and several loose white mushrooms. "Uh, Magda, what do I do?"

"Here, I printed these out for you." She handed him a stack of papers covering everything from the history of Garden Hermits to a Wikipedia page of druid rituals to fortune telling. "This should cover you. You've just gotta keep it up for a month or two. She'll move onto the next project soon."

Magdalena opened that damned gold fridge and grabbed a bottle of cold brew. She'd been awake since three am, worrying about her son attending college in California who hadn't called her in two months.

"What do you mean?" asked Richie as he tugged on the neck of his long robe. And Magdalena thought her starchy black uniform was hot.

"You're the new peacocks." She sat in an overstuffed floral armchair. Perhaps this hermit wasn't all bad. His house provided her with a place to rest. And a spot far from Debra's constant requests. That woman was a black hole of need. Get too close and she sucked you into providing something. A turmeric superfood smoothie. A pair of handmade leather sandals from the island of Capri. Assurances that her $700 eye cream was really working.

It was also a haven from Duke, a black hole of a darker kind, whose patrician exterior belied his ugly core. First it had been a whispered warning from Inga, the baby nurse, that Duke had yelled at her when Philip's diaper had leaked on the antique Persian rug in the nursery. Then it was the hole in the wall of Duke's office he claimed was from a book falling off a shelf, but was clearly from his fist. Magdalena's strategy was to avoid Duke as much as possible, which wasn't hard because he was often traveling for his job. And when he was at home, he was most often holed up in his office doing that nebulous "work" which comprised moving colossal sums of money around.

"Two years ago she bought thirty Indian peacocks to live on the property. They shit everywhere and chased anyone who visited the house."

"Sounds like something out of a movie." Richie grinned, and Magdalena noticed he was missing two of his bottom molars.

She could tell Richie was not the type of guy to demand his espresso be exactly 93° Celsius.

"And before that was the grand piano she never learned how to play and the racehorse she insisted would be a Kentucky Derby Champion. I thought the baby would keep her busy, but after a couple weeks she found out babies are fun to hold for ten minutes before they need something. Anyway, the woman has too much time on her hands and more money than God." Magdalena knew it was a risk talking so openly to Richie, but she wished someone had spoken to her this frankly when she had first been plunged into working for the ultra-wealthy. She would never forget the shock she felt when her first employer had purchased a hotel chain because he enjoyed his room service coq au vin. She'd always thought rich people flew first class and drove foreign cars. But the gap between the 1% and the .1% was an enormous crevasse stuffed with offshore accounts and immigrant sweat.

Why would he take this job? Who gives up a year of their life to be a glorified garden gnome? But when she reflected on her own motivations for working for the Frechettes, she knew what Richie's motivation had been. Money. This one year of hermit work was probably more money than he'd made in the last ten years combined. But that wasn't all of it. He must have a plan for the $200,000. A great need that was worth jumping through all the hoops of getting hired and spending a year of his life in this ornamental cabin assuring Mrs. Frechette that the stars would smile upon her girl's trip to Lake Como.

"So what would your advice be?" he asked.

"It's like any job. Always look busy." She drained her cold brew and threw the glass bottle in the tree stump shaped trash can. "What did you do before this, Richie?"

"Oh, um," he stared at the fairy mural on the wall as though it might give him the answer to this innocuous question, "You think those are fairies or pixies? I don't know the difference, but I bet…"

"For a job, I mean. What was your profession?" Why was he being so cagey? Perhaps this bumbling old man had something to hide.

"This and that." He fiddled with the copper orb, pushing it back and forth across the counter.

Magdalena's imagination went into overdrive. Maybe he was on the run from the law. Or a federal agent investigating Mr. Frechette. She had always suspected those flashy charitable donations were a way to avoid paying taxes. Or Richie had testified against a drug kingpin and was now hiding out, waiting for the day the kingpin's men knocked on his door in the middle of the night. Or… she looked at Richie's callused hands and sun spotted forehead; he was a down-on-his-luck pensioner looking for an easy payday.

"You have kids?" she asked. Maybe he'd taken the job for his kids. As someone who spent her life catering to the whims of the wealthy so her sons could go to college with their children, she understood that motivation.

He nodded. Okay, she was getting somewhere.

"Boy or girl?"

"A daughter. Lennie. Er, Helena, now that she's grown." Richie's voice softened and he stopped fiddling with the copper orb.

"That's a lovely name."

"One good thing I gave her. I met her momma at Wild Hog Saloon in Helena, Arkansas. I always joked that if she'd been a boy, we'd have named her Wild Hog instead."

"That's funny. My parents named me after where they met. Magdalena. A town up in Laguna Province. I don't even remember it. We moved to America when I was two and they moved back when I was eighteen." She had missed her parents terribly for the eight years they'd lived in Manila, then even more terribly when they died. "I'm sure Helena misses you. A year is a long time to be away."

"Oh, we don't talk. The last time I saw her she must have been, twelve? Thirteen? Around the time her mom married a man who didn't drink his paychecks the moment he got 'em." He grinned; the pain far enough gone the tragedy had become funny. "I blew through town. I think I took her to McDonald's. Yeah, must have been because she wanted a McRib. But they didn't have them. She wasn't even surprised. Like she expected to be disappointed."

Magdalena nodded. She had also missed most of her sons' childhoods while she was working. The sting of picking her boys up from school and having to show ID proving she was their mother because no one at the school recognized her. She tried to offer a comforting platitude. "I'm sure she…"

"What happened to the peacocks?" he asked.

"What?" The moment was gone.

"The peacocks. You said there were thirty living here, but I haven't seen one."

Magdalena pointed to the ceiling where hundreds of peacock feathers were glued on in elaborate swirls. Tenants who had overstayed their welcome.

❖ ❖ ❖

"Good evening, Martlebaum," Debra said as she knocked on the cabin door. José had outdone himself with these flowers. It smelled exactly like the Connecticut Flower & Garden Show, which her family had sponsored for the past forty years.

Martlebaum opened the door. He looked as though he'd stepped right out of the illustration in her coffee-table book.

"Good evening, Mrs. Frechette," he said, bowing.

"Those robes look incredible, Martlebaum." Paying extra for an Italian tailor had been worth it.

"Thank you. Your dress is lovely, as well."

"You like it?" She smoothed her light blue lace dress. "Kate Middleton has the same one. You know, we were born in the same month. Capricorn sisters. How are you finding everything in your new home?"

"It's all very nice, ma'am." He looked at her expectantly.

"Did Magdalena give you your supplies?"

"Yes, ma'am."

"She's great, isn't she? That Filipina work ethic."

"Yes, ma'am."

"Um, yes… ah." Why was she so nervous? This was *her* Garden Hermit. Debra had spent all this time and money to acquire a Garden Hermit and had no idea what to do with him. "Red or purple?"

"Pardon?"

"Choose a color Martlebaum. Red or purple?"

"Hm, red."

Another excruciating silence.

"Is there anything else I can help you with, ma'am?"

Why was this so difficult? No, she was being too hard on herself. Compassion was her word of the day. "We're having friends over Friday night for dinner and I thought it was the perfect moment for you to make your debut."

"Yes, ma'am."

"And Martlebaum, I promise I'll prepare more for our next visit. You know, I'll-"

"The heart can only speak when it's ready, ma'am." He touched her lightly on the arm. "Have a good evening."

Debra's heart thumped in her chest at Martlebaum's wise words. She had been right about him.

◆ ◆ ◆

Buffy Hawthorne wasn't a woman to turn down a third glass of wine. Especially not at one of her husband's interminable business dinners. Why business couldn't be done during daylight hours without getting lobster Thermidor and wives involved was beyond her comprehension. At least the Frechettes were close by, only an hour's drive from Manhattan. And Debra Frechette loved nothing more than the sound of a neck creaking as it nodded along with her stream of speech, allowing Buffy to sip her wine in near silence.

"What a meal," said Buffy's husband, Kenneth. She loved him despite hating everything he did and said. "I'll have Nick email those contracts over on Monday."

"Excellent," said the Frechette husband. Buffy couldn't remember his name.

"We'd better be hitting the road," said Kenneth, pushing his chair back from the table. A housekeeper appeared with their coats.

"No, wait," shouted Debra springing up from the table, "I have a surprise for you. Put on your coats and I'll take you."

"Honey, the Hawthornes are already out the door," said the husband.

"It'll only take a minute. Buffy will love it." Debra's bracelets desperately jangled on her skinny arms as she tried to gesticulate Buffy toward enthusiasm.

Kenneth was texting the driver to pull around. Or texting his side piece about their weekend romp at The Carlyle. A moment of not getting what he wanted wouldn't hurt him.

"Oh yes, Debra, I'd love to see your surprise." Buffy dashed to Debra's side, locking arms like schoolgirls. The husbands followed them into the night, down a stone path toward a little house. It was cute, in a rustic way, with twinkly lights and a thatched roof.

Debra grabbed Buffy's shoulders and stopped her at the edge of a cobblestone circle in front of the house. The men stopped behind her, Debra's husband apologizing under his breath. Buffy thought the charming house was the surprise and was about to congratulate Debra on her architectural achievement when she heard a rustling in the trees to the left of the house. A bearded man in a long dark robe peeked out from behind a tree. He looked to be about sixty, but Buffy had trouble telling the ages of people who hadn't used adequate sun protection in their youth.

"Ooh, it's Martlebaum," said Debra, as if everyone should know what she was talking about. Buffy clapped, regretting agreeing to whatever this was going to be.

"Greetings travelers," said the man in the robes, "What brings you to the home of wise old Martlebaum?" The man stepped into the clearing, supporting himself with a branch he used as a walking stick.

"What the fuck," muttered Kenneth. His disdain spurred Buffy into action.

"Hi Martlebaum, I'm Buffy Hawthorne." She stuck out a hand. He shook it, and when she pulled away, she had a small white mushroom in her palm.

"Ask him something," said Debra. "He's very wise. He helped me pick out this dress." She gestured to the red cocktail dress Buffy had insincerely complimented.

"Um, I'm not sure." She met Martlebaum's gaze. It was a patient look. No anger at her for stumbling over her words or threat if she said the wrong thing. At no point did his eyes appraise the size of her ring or the slimness of her waist. The last living thing that had looked at her with such tolerance had been her childhood dog, Belle.

"That's all right, Buffy," Martlebaum said, "If we don't know the question, it means we already know the answer."

Buffy's lip quivered. She did have all the answers. Martlebaum pulled a horse's skull out of the bottom of the babbling fountain. He placed it in front of Buffy. She knew what to do. She bent down and put the mushroom into the horse's mouth. Then she turned to her husband and met his gaze. It was all judgment, and she knew he'd mock her pitilessly in the car for participating in Debra's kooky show. But right now, all that mattered was the confidence swelling in her chest.

"I want," Buffy paused on the edge, deciding how high of a cliff she was about to throw herself off. A baby? A tattoo? A divorce? "A dog."

"Uh, sure. I'll have Esperanza make a list of breeders in the morning. Can we go now?" He yawned into his elbow.

Buffy didn't look back at Martlebaum as she led her husband to the car.

Magdalena needed a cigarette. They were officially banned from the Frechette home for their cancerous stench. She knew Duke kept a secret pack on the back porch, but she couldn't risk getting caught stealing. And he probably smoked something fancy and strange. Magdalena preferred Marlboro Menthol Gold. Cool, minty smoke along with the pleasant buzz of nicotine was what she needed after spending an entire morning standing in front of the house waiting on the delivery of a rare orchid. Normally, a lower level staff member could take the job of waiting, but this Gold of Kinabalu orchid was a gift from Mr. Frechette's mother and Debra was still new enough to her marriage that she cared what her mother-in-law thought of her. Magdalena remembered the feeling. The anxiety that had caused her to cook four types of pie at Thanksgiving to be sure there was one her mother-in-law would enjoy. She had joked that her husband was lucky Magdalena's parents had moved back to Manila and could only judge him from eight thousand miles away. But that was the past. Both her husband and mother-in-law had been gone for twenty years. Taken out by a drunk driver who swerved onto the wrong side of the road.

But the orchid never came. A customs snafu at JFK. Magdalena was supposed to be on the phone with the Malaysian consulate, arguing for the civil rights of a stupid flower. And she would be. But there was no reason she couldn't listen to Malaysian hold music while taking a walk in the woods. The gardening staff kept the tree line that touched the western edge of the Frechette's massive estate neatly trimmed, but ten feet in, Magdalena could almost forget she was at work. She tramped through brush with her black orthopedic shoes. She remembered bringing her sons out to play in the woods behind their apartment complex, treating the small stand of trees like a vast unexplored fantasy forest.

"And will she be able to do it? Will Magda the Magnificent be able to trick the evil customs officials and get the magic orchid safely into the hands of Princess Frechette?" She held out her cell phone like a sword. "Will she-"

Snap!

Magdalena scanned the trees. Was it a black bear? A bobcat? A skunk? No. It was a Garden Hermit. Richie sheepishly approached her, his long robe catching on the underbrush.

"Didn't mean to scare you," he said, "I was taking a walk and heard a voice. Thought I'd stretch my legs. Get away for a bit." His eyes were bright. He looked the happiest Magdalena had seen him, out here in the wild.

"It's fine. I came out here for a break too." She kicked a fallen tree, determined the trunk was solid, and sat down. Richie stayed standing, pacing the forest like a dog off his leash. "Well, not really a break. I have to make a phone call."

"Don't let me bother you," he said as he walked back into the trees.

She pulled her phone from her pocket and had an idea. "Richie, wait." He turned, and she held up her cellphone. "I know you're not supposed to use technology, but out here, no one will know. Is there anyone you want to call?"

"Oh, I don't... Mrs. Frechette said... I shouldn't."

"It'll be fine. This is my personal phone." When Debra hired her, she offered her a place on the staff phone plan. She'd refused saying she didn't want to kick her sons off her family plan. Which was true. But she also didn't want the Frechettes poring over her call logs or reading her text messages. Not that there was anything bad, but she valued any privacy she could get in the Frechette panopticon.

"Well," he said tugging his beard, "If you don't mind."

She handed him her phone, and he dialed the number.

"The number you dialed has been changed, disconnected, or is no longer in service. If you feel you have-" said the robotic voice on the other end of the line. Richie winced and hung up.

"Thanks," he said. He handed the phone back and walked into the forest.

"I can try another number," she said, but he was already gone.

"I visited yesterday afternoon, and you weren't here." Debra and her hermit sat on the stone bench outside of his house eating lunch, him a turkey sandwich and her a can of Pamplemousse La Croix.

"I went for a walk. I'm sorry, ma'am." He looked contrite, so Debra withheld her scolding.

"It's fine, Martlebaum. I was thinking about what you said, about my heart speaking when it's ready, and I'm ready to talk."

Martlebaum put down his sandwich and waited for her to begin.

"Did you know we used to have peacocks? It was before you got here. Another one of my projects."

He stayed silent, nodding along as she spoke.

"I've always been this way, diving into one thing headfirst then moving on. The fencing lessons or learning French or saving the Pandas. It's exhausting. I wish I could be like you, Martlebaum. Living a quiet insignificant life. Satisfied by the simple things. Look at you. Eating a sandwich on white bread as if it's beluga caviar."

"There is more satisfaction in giving than in any other human action."

And there it was, plain as day. Debra needed to throw a party.

◆ ◆ ◆

Duke Frechette stepped over a plastic skeleton laying on the porch, waiting to be strung up by the decorating team his wife had hired for her Halloween party. Inside, his tasteful home was being festooned with pentagrams, jack-o'-lanterns, and iron cages containing live owls. In the middle of it all his wife was directing workers who were raising a devil made of antlers above their fireplace.

"I thought we agreed no more live birds," he said.

"We agreed not to *buy* any more live birds. The owls are rented." She walked over and slipped her hands under his jacket, stroking up and down his ribs. "It's Philip's first Halloween. Will you please stay for the party?"

He'd been making flimsy allusions to "business" he needed to do in the city ever since his wife had slipped the 3-D haunted house invitation on his desk. Usually, she went all out for their annual Christmas party, but he knew she wanted to show off the weird old man she had living in the shed. Though Duke had misgivings about every single one of his wife's projects, he tried to be supportive. He hadn't been supportive of his first wife, and now he paid $30,000 a month for her to live in a wellness commune in the desert to "recover her inner light."

Women were like rabbits. Rabbits are masters of hiding illness and distress. One moment they're happy and healthy, hopping around the yard, and the next they've flopped down dead. Rich, sheltered women were experts at concealing their pain and resentment until you found them passed out in the bathroom with their stomachs full of white wine and Percocet. If the parties and the strange hobbies kept Debra hopping, he'd keep footing the bill.

"Ok, I'll come to the party. But I'm not-"

"We're going to be Titania and Oberon, and Philip will be Puck. Your robe is on our bed, if you want to try it on."

At least a fairy king robe would be comfortable. "What's, um, Martlebaum going to be doing?"

Debra tapped the tip of his nose. "You'll have to wait and see, mister."

"If you clone the dog then you'll never have to say good-bye," said Kenneth Hawthorne as Han Solo, sipping a glass of boozy witch's brew.

"But he won't be the same dog, just a copy," slurred Buffy, a sloppy Snow White.

"Well, that depends if you believe in nature vs. nurture. I read in The Times..."

Despite getting dragged into this awful conversation, Debra's Halloween party was going off without a hitch. Friends drank and danced, had their pictures taken by the professional photographer, ate gourmet spooky canapes, and had caricatures carved into pumpkins. A server dressed as a pirate passed her and Debra grabbed a puff pastry mummy from his tray.

The clock struck ten, and the guide summoned twenty more party guests to Martlebaum's home to take part in a real Druid ritual. The guests who had returned from the ritual had been lavishing her with praise.

"Unlike anything I've ever experienced."

"I swear I saw a ghost coming out of the bonfire."

"I'm not a believer, but that hermit is magic."

It felt good to share his wisdom with others. She'd never felt as though anything she'd done had weight. Her words lacked the heft of experience, but through Martlebaum she could feel wise.

Under the Day of the Dead face paint, Debra recognized her friend Mimi, whose gift had been the inspiration to acquire a Garden Hermit in the first place. Debra and Mimi were friends in the way a cobra and a mongoose were friends. There were many high-quality images of them together with bared teeth.

"Mimi," squealed Debra, "I'm so glad you could make it. I'm so sorry about Peter."

Mimi's husband Peter had left her for their Norwegian au pair. Really, it was Mimi's fault for being the first wife. Men needed to go through one expensive divorce before they could make a marriage work.

Mimi flicked open her black lace fan, aggressively moving the air between them. "As long as I get the Rembrandt and the house in the Hamptons, I'll be happy. Where is your husband?"

Debra had seen Duke retreat to his office an hour ago. "My Oberon is off mingling. I wanted to thank you for your gift. That book on gardens was so inspirational."

"Oh, that? My cousin was the publisher. Sent me two boxes. But I'm glad you enjoyed it." Mimi's eyes roved over the party, searching for something to criticize. "You know, I heard owls carry this disease that-"

"Mimi!" She pulled her toward the group of guests headed outside for Martlebaum's ten o'clock ritual. "Let's go outside. I have something to show you."

Mimi's face itched. The professional face painter had assured her the paint was organic and allergen free, but Mimi suspected the bitch had been lying. At least Mimi hadn't tipped.

And now she was standing outside of a tacky cabin

around a bonfire, waiting for Debra's show. Mimi was about to comment that she'd seen better looking cabins in Thomas Kinkade paintings, when a man emerged from the forest holding a lantern. Wow, a knock-off Gandalf.

"Hoof and horn, hoof and horn," said the man.

"Hoof and horn, hoof and horn," replied the group around the bonfire.

"All that dies shall be reborn."

"All that dies shall be reborn," said Mimi, louder and more sarcastically than anyone else in the circle.

"Corn and grain, corn and grain."

"Corn and grain, corn and grain."

"All that falls shall rise again."

"All that falls shall rise again."

Jesus, were people buying this bullshit?

"Tonight is the festival of Samhain," said the man in robes, "The one night of the year when the veil between our world and the world of the spirits is the thinnest. Through our ritual, we have lifted this veil. But spirits do not enter the mortal realm willingly. For us to commune with them, we must first show them we are willing to give something in return." He held up a golden chalice. "I shall mark you with this, the blood of a goat, as a signal of your sacrifice."

"It's real goat's blood," whispered Debra. "Humanely harvested, of course."

The man walked around the circle muttering and dabbing blood on each party guest's forehead. When he reached Mimi, he dipped a finger into the blood and raised it to her forehead. She let him do it, grinning as the blood dripped down her face.

"Good job last night," said Magdalena as she loaded fresh produce into Richie's fridge. "You were the highlight of the party."

"For a ritual cribbed from Wikipedia, it went all right."

Richie took an apple from the bowl of fruit. "You know, this hermit thing is fun. Most days I take walks or read books or try writing poetry. And all while eating the best food I've ever had in my life and getting paid for it. You can't tell because of the robes, but since I've gotten here, I've put on twenty pounds."

"If you need more, I've got ten on each hip you can have." She shut the fridge door and joined Richie at the glittering marble table decorated with real butterfly wings.

"You know, sometimes I feel lousy, like I'm taking advantage by getting all this for doing nothing, but then–"

"You remember the Frechettes are billionaires?" finished Magdalena. Her pager buzzed, summoning her to the big house. "Don't feel guilty. Their monthly budget for candles is more than I make in a year. Don't feel bad for taking what they don't need."

A year ago, Katya would have said there were no ugly babies. Every single one was a gift from God and was beautiful for having been created in his image. But Philip Frechette was an ugly baby. She'd taken a surreptitious picture on her cellphone and sent it to her boyfriend. He had replied that the baby resembled Nosferatu. With his big ears and pinched face, Katya had to agree.

The baby monitor in her pocket wailed and she went upstairs to check on the miniature vampyr. As she passed Duke's office, she heard yelling. Normally, she had the discretion to ignore her employer's marital disputes, but the words "worshipping Satan" drifted through the door and she had to listen in.

"It's not good for business, honey. I can't have clients believe I'm sacrificing goats in the backyard." He slammed his laptop shut with such ferocity the screen shattered. "I got an email from Alan our lawyer asking why he wasn't invited to our masked orgy."

"But nothing like that happened," said Debra, on the verge

of tears.

"And worst of all," he said, picking up a letter opener and stabbing it into his walnut desk, "my mother called and asked if we were still planning on raising Philip as a Catholic."

"It's a rumor, Duke. It'll pass."

"That's where it starts. I already squashed a blog post about the ad in the Penny Saver. I've been thinking and I'm not sure if it's a good look for us to be employing a man to be our garden ornament."

"A good look? What is that supposed-"

"It's all optics. You treat him well, but imagine if the press-"

"Since when did you care about the press?"

"You know, hatred of the wealthy is the last acceptable form of discrimination. Remember those hooligans who threw ranch dressing on me and screamed eat the rich? We're getting rid of him Debra. And we can do it your way or my way and I know which one Martlebaum would prefer."

"Knock-knock, Martlebaum," said Debra as she waited at his door. After taking off her makeup, crying for an hour, then reapplying her makeup, she was ready to tell Martlebaum the tragic news.

"Good afternoon, ma'am. You look... oh, Mrs. Frechette, what's wrong?"

Of course he could tell she was upset. He was her loyal, kind Martlebaum.

"Duke, Duke he wants... he told me." Martlebaum guided her into his living room and let her lay on the moss green couch. "I don't know what I'm going to do without you. I've betrayed you." The ground was dissolving beneath her feet. She clutched Martlebaum's soft black robe, the only thing keeping her from dissolving with it.

◆ ◆ ◆

Duke had made a mistake. He never should have demanded the hermit's removal. Foolish rumors would pass, but the blankness in his wife's eyes would not. It was a terrifying echo to the first Mrs. Frechette. But this time he would not let her hide her sadness until it was too late.

They sat at the dinner table picking at their salmon while the baby nurse tried to get Philip to eat mashed peas. After the third glop of peas hit the floor Duke said, "Katya, could you please take him upstairs."

"Come on, Drac," said Katya as she scooped up the baby and took him away.

Both spoke at the same time.

"I'm not-"

"I thought-"

"Can I go first?" asked Duke. "It was wrong to tell you to get rid of Martlebaum. He's special to you and I'm very sorry."

Debra exhaled and fanned at her eyes. "I'm so happy to hear you say that Duke."

Here it was. The shiny new toy to dangle in front of his wife's eyes. He'd proposed to her at the top of the Eiffel Tower and she'd asked if they could move to Paris after they were married. He'd said no, citing the inconvenience of running a business in a different time zone. But now, being across the ocean from the hermit was convenient indeed.

"Let's move to Paris." Before she could respond, he knelt beside her. "You can go shopping and look at art and Philip can learn French. He'll pick it up like a sponge."

"Duke, don't tease. You know it's my dream." Her huge blue eyes welled up with tears. "You're going to make me cry out my lash extensions."

"Will Paris make you happy?"

"More than anything."

"Then we'll go."

She kissed him. "I'm calling Fiona. She and her husband rented a place right along the Seine. I have to get her realtor's number." She kissed him again then ran up the stairs.

Duke had never spoken to the hermit. The lawyer had done a background check to make sure he wasn't a child diddling axe murderer, but other than that Duke knew nothing about the man who had been living on his property for four months. The hermit was sitting outside on a stone bench reading a book.

"Nice night," said Duke.

"Yes sir," replied the hermit. He closed the book and smiled at Duke.

"We're moving to Paris." Duke sat on the opposite bench very aware the hermit had not offered him a seat.

The hermit nodded.

"It because of you, Martle...fuck, what's your actual name?"

"Richie."

"My wife and I have to pack up our lives and move to Paris because of you. You and your show at Halloween. I know my wife didn't come up with the idea to do a Satanic ritual for our closest friends. That came from your sick little mind." Duke poked his finger hard into the hermit's chest. "You. You're worse than the fucking peacocks. At least with them I could get José to put rat poison in their food. But I can't do that to you, can I?"

The hermit stayed silent.

"Or fuck, I probably could. Any man who can afford to leave everything behind for an entire year to be a human lawn ornament doesn't have much going for him on the outside." Duke pulled a cigarette case from his jacket and lit one. "So here's my question, why would someone degrade themselves for a year? Put on woo-woo magic shows and dress like a wizard. Why?"

The hermit grinned. "Are you serious?"

How dare this costumed fuck talk back to him. This insolent piece of shit who'd been living in his yard like a stray dog. Duke grabbed the hermit's arm and pressed the lit cigarette into his flesh. He screamed as his arm burned. There. The hermit wasn't smiling any longer. Duke pulled out another cigarette and lit it. The hermit stood up, clutching at his burnt arm.

"Fuck man. What is wrong- Money! I agreed to do this whole song and dance for money. What other possible fucking reason would I have for-"

"Shut up, I'm thinking." He shouldn't have burnt him. That had been an overreaction. The hermit was dangerous. Who knew what secrets his wife had been telling this hermit and now Duke had left him with a scar? He could see the headlines now, *Out of Touch Billionaires Abuse Human Garden Gnome.*

"I'm sorry."

The hermit didn't respond. He was bent over, gasping in pain, holding a hand over the burn on his arm.

"While we are abroad, a part of the staff will stay here to keep the house running. You will be on that list. You will continue to do your hermit duties until your contract expires then will be given your full salary. If you leave before then, you will not receive any money. Is that understood?"

"So I keep doing this? Even when you aren't here?"

"You agreed to a year of work and I will have a year of work. Agreed?"

"Yes, agreed."

Duke almost stuck out his hand for a handshake, but thought better of it. He put out his cigarette on the stone bench. There. Another problem solved.

Richie picked up a double chocolate muffin from the plate on his counter, twisted off the stump, and threw it in the trash. In a few short months he'd gone from a man who attended Bible study groups for the free donuts to someone who didn't think twice about only eating half of a gourmet pastry. The Frechettes had moved to Paris a month ago. Mrs. Frechette hadn't even said goodbye, which, if Richie was honest with himself, had stung. To be thrown out like last season's Gucci heels. Though he comforted himself with the fact that there was nothing wrong with three month old shoes, just as there was nothing wrong with him. Disposability lay in the eye of the beholder.

Richie's life had settled into a comfortable routine. Not that life hadn't been comfortable before, what with his primary duty being to say vague things to make Mrs. Frechette feel better about whatever decision she had already made. But this was a whole other level of comfort.

He slept in until ten, ate filet mignon, watched TV on the laptop Magdalena had snuck him, read books, played solitaire, went for walks, fed the squirrels, napped in the sun, joked with the guys on the garden crew, watched a meteor shower, built a snowman, watched the sunrise from his roof, drew landscapes, collected bird feathers, taught himself how to make crepes, meditated, and completed a thousand piece jigsaw puzzle of a puppy asleep next to a crackling fire.

And before he knew it, he had been living his hermit life for a year. Though the house was kept ready for their return, the Frechettes never came back. He had heard from Magdalena that Mrs. Frechette had purchased an apartment once owned by Coco Chanel and was throwing herself into renovations. And when Duke visited for business, he stayed at their penthouse in New York, which was closer to his office. Richie was glad they never visited. He didn't want to encounter Duke's temper again, and he wasn't sure how much longer his wise old man act would have held up to Mrs. Frechette's increasing need for mystical advice.

◆ ◆ ◆

On a bright summer day, Magdalena knocked on Richie's door.

"Come on in," he yelled from the couch where he was reading a book. Once a month Magdalena brought him a bag of books from the Frechette's massive library. Even after a year he hadn't made a dent.

"Hey Richie. Hot enough for you?"

"I prefer ninety degrees to nine."

"That's fair." She grabbed a Coke from the fridge and joined him in the living room. "The Frechettes are staying in Paris."

Richie sat up.

"Don't worry, they aren't selling this place. They promoted me to house manager here. All I'm saying is nothing's going to change, if you want to stay. The last time I talked to Mrs. Frechette, she was trying to find an exact match to the paint Coco Chanel used to paint her apartment in 1965. I don't think she even remembers you exist."

"Oh, that's good. Better than the alternative."

"The alternative?"

Richie pointed at the ceiling where peacock feathers swirled.

"Lena, there's an envelope for you," yelled Grover from the entryway.

"Bring the mail in here. This macaroni keeps trying to boil over." Helena had eyeballed the amount of water for the double batch of Kraft macaroni and cheese and her eyeballs had betrayed her.

"Put a wooden spoon on top," said Grover, kissing her on the cheek and handing her the mail. "It'll stop the bubbles from forming."

"My Iron Chef." She took the mail from him and sat at the kitchen table. Utility bill, People Magazine, Little Caesar coupon, and a thick envelope with a fancy law firm as the return address.

"You aren't divorcing me, are you?" joked Grover, joining her at the table. "Because if you want to take half of my Marvel

Legends you'll need-"

"It's a check for two hundred thousand dollars." The paper shook in Helena's trembling hand.

"What? For real?"

"No, it's gotta be a scam."

Grover picked up the letter enclosed with the check. "It says it's for the work of Richard Allen. Do you know who that is?"

She did.

"You're staying?"

"Yes. I don't have anywhere better to be."

"Oh I'm sure you-"

"I've been reading online about hermits. Lots of sinners leave society to seek spiritual enlightenment. This year has been the longest I've ever gone without hurting or disappointing or screwing over anyone in my entire life. I'm not doing anyone any good here, but being a neutral presence in the world is a hell of a lot better than how I'd been living my life before."

"That's lovely, Richie."

The air grew too sincere. "And I've gotten used to having a shelf full of macarons. I won't get that back in Mattoon."

"I checked with the lawyer and Helena Franklin cashed her check last week."

"Thank you, Magda."

And for a while they sat in the shade, Richie reading his book and Magdalena texting her son. When the sun faded behind the trees, Magdalena went back to the big house and Richie returned to his small house. He lay on his silk canopy bed and watched the fairy mobile spin, propelled by the wind from his open window. As the fairies did their tinkling dance, he sank into the down comforter. Tucked away from the world he had never felt more a part of.

Yes, Of Course, I'm Satisfied By Just The Tip Of This Piece Of Cheesecake

Dessert? After three whole bites of my wedge salad and half a yeasted roll? I simply couldn't. I'm absolutely stuffed. Filled to the brim. If one more ounce of matter entered my body, I'd explode like a meat and blood supernova, spraying everyone in this Ruth's Chris Steak House with my assorted viscera. Even if I spent the rest of eternity in a cryogenically induced slumber, I could never dream of taking one more bite.

Well, if Mr. Steve-I'll-Be-Your-Waiter-This-Evening has already brought the dessert menu... it would be rude not to at least look it over.

And of course, you should order a dessert, my virile lover. After watching you polish off the entire breadbasket, two lobster tails, a 40 oz ribeye, and Idaho's largest baked potato, I know you'd love to finish your gastronomic maelstrom with something sweet. Sure, you've shamelessly enjoyed a delectable orgy of indulgence while saying, "Do you really need those carbs?" when I glanced toward the breadbasket. But you're a man! A man who doesn't have to consider his consumption in public because his body is not up for public consumption.

Let me see. Chocolate sin cake? Bread pudding? Crème brûlée? Those are all a bit... heavy. I'll have the tip of a slice of vanilla cheesecake.

I assure you Mr. Steve-You-Can-Add-Six-Jumbo-Shrimp-To-Your-Entree-For-Fifteen-Dollars, bringing out an entire human-sized serving of cheesecake would be an abominable waste. You'd serve me the creamy triangle, and I'd hem and haw about how much SoulCycle I'll need to do to burn this off. My masculine dinner companion would assure me I'm beautiful no matter my size. But when he zipped up my dress earlier this

135

evening, he pinched my back fat in what seemed like a playful gesture but was in reality a silent reprimand.

I'd run my fork through the whipped topping, playfully sucking on the tines. Yummm, I'd moan. I'm so bad. Then I'd take the fork and cut off the tiniest tip of the cheesecake slice. Maybe half an inch. In no society on Earth would the amount of cheesecake on my fork be considered a bite, but I'd open my mouth wide enough for a semi-truck to park between my tonsils. I'd deposit the cheesecake tip on my tongue, such a small bite I'd barely get a hint of a wisp of vanilla before it dissolved down my throat. But by the sounds of pleasure I'd emit, everyone in this dimly lit steakery would think I'd had a squirting howling labia blasting five-alarm orgasm.

Timidly, I'd push away the plate. So embarrassed my date spent ten whole dollars on this dessert and I'm such a dainty baby lady I could barely gulp down a single bite. In a voice higher than Betty Boop on helium, I'd ask if he could help me... finish it? He'd scoop the 99% intact piece of cheesecake onto his plate. "Thank you for helping me finish," I'd lie for the first of three times this evening. He'd smile approvingly at me, digging into his orgy of indulgence as I sipped my diet vodka soda.

So that's why, Mr. Steve-Ruth's-Is-A-Possessive-So-The-Name-Does-Make-Sense, I just want the tip of a slice of vanilla cheesecake.

Actually, never mind.

Just talking about the micro-sliver of New York Style perdition has satisfied my sweet tooth. Sure, as you serve my beard stubble calloused penis of a man with his dessert, you'll hear my stomach audibly rumble. Maybe because I'm so hungry I'm hallucinating that my purse is a dancing honey-baked ham? Maybe because the last time I ate dessert without guilt was a slice of my fifth birthday cake? Maybe because I've been bombarded with so many external messages to make myself as small as possible that I think it's actually my idea, appointing myself warden of my own personal patriarchal prison?

Who can say? Certainly not me. My brain can't come to

any conclusions because I've only consumed enough calories today to support the functioning of a below-average toddler.

And Now A Word From Our Sponsors

Penny Pinching Tips for the Morally Bankrupt
is also brought to you by

Broatmeal: *Oatmeal for Men.*

A jacked dude in a ripped t-shirt bursts out of bed.

Men, do you have this problem? You wake up in the morning and you're hungry, but breakfast is for pussies.

He punches Captain Crunch in the stomach.

That's why I invented Broatmeal, Oatmeal for Men. No need to cook it like a woman, you just jam the raw Broatmeal into your manhole.

In a kitchen, he pulls a metal jar decorated with flames from the cabinet. He has never cried before.

With all the kick-ass nutrition you need to man-power your man-engine.

Closeup of the Broatmeal. It is uncooked oatmeal with marshmallows in the shapes of manly things i.e. cars, boobs, guns.

Spoons? Bowls? What are you, a utensil loving cuck? Every can of Broatmeal comes with the only utensil you need, a machete.

He pulls a machete from a drawer, shoveling the Broatmeal into his mouth. It spills down his t-shirt and tinkles on the floor. One time he masturbated so hard his penis ripped a little from his body.

Our mascot isn't a lame-ass Quaker in a hat.

He punches the Quaker Oats Man in the throat.

It's Brett Kavanaugh on a jet ski.

We see a shot of Brett Kavanaugh slicing manatees on a jet ski. Then back to the man choking down the dry Broatmeal. He has never made a woman laugh or cum.

Buy Broatmeal today and eat breakfast like a man.

*Use promo code PINCH30 for 30% off your purchase of a month's supply of Broatmeal. Order in the next five minutes and receive a limited edition Brett Kavanaugh bobble head.

Choose Your Own Adventure: Seducing The Earl At Lady Worthingham's Masquerade Ball

London, 1760. You have been invited to Lady Worthingham's glamorous masquerade ball. Though your family is fabulously wealthy, you will inherit nothing if you are not married. Tonight, you must secure a proposal of marriage from the kind and handsome Earl of Collinwood if you hope to avoid marriage to your father's business associate, the loathsome Baron Mortimer.

Will you secure the Earl's hand? **(1)**
Or drink the vial of poison on your nightstand? **(2)**

◆ ◆ ◆

(1) Your maids dress you in your shift, side hoops, petticoat, corset, grey silk gown, and tie it together with your jeweled stomacher. A maid brings in two masks for you to wear to the ball. You disguise yourself as...

A tiger **(3)**
A peacock **(4)**

◆ ◆ ◆

(3) Disguised as the Queen of the Jungle you arrive at the ball. Devils and angels, harlequins and harlots, beasts and beauties, drink and dance in the ornate ballroom. A Count may be disguised as a humble fool, a woman of ill repute concealed in a nun's habit. The debauched atmosphere engulfs you, but you must stay true to your task. A servant offers you three drinks. You take a...

Flute of champagne? **(5)**
Glass of wine? **(6)**
Cup of water? **(7)**

◆ ◆ ◆

(2) The maid brings in your dress for the ball, but finds you lifeless on the bed. Ashamed of your suicide, your family pays a gravedigger to take you away and bury you at once. You awaken in a coffin. You...

Scratch at the lid of the coffin. **(8)**
Scream for help. **(9)**

◆ ◆ ◆

(8) You break through the lid and dig your way out of your grave. The cemetery keeper sees you emerge and asks if you want to go home. You say...

Yes. Take me home. **(10)**
No. Let's get married. **(11)**

◆ ◆ ◆

(5) WHORE! Bubbling liquids are the Devil dancing on a lady's tongue. The Earl of Collinwood sees you sipping your slut juice and immediately proposes to your rival, Lady Eastaughffe. You marry Baron Mortimer and bear him seven terrible sons.

◆ ◆ ◆

(9) All day and night you scream, but in 18th century London women's screams are as common as birdsong and you

141

are ignored. You use up all the oxygen in the coffin and suffocate.

(7) FOOL! This is 18th century London. The water isn't fit for human consumption. You spend all night in the lavatory, unable to seduce anyone but the toilet. Baron Mortimer hears of your illness and refuses to marry you. You are promised to an Italian noble, but on the journey to Italy you perish from Consumption you caught from the toilet.

(10) The cemetery keeper takes you back to your family's home. Your father opens the door and faints from shock. Believing you have demonic powers, your family does not force you to marry and your father agrees to split the inheritance evenly among his children, securing your future. You take your money, move to Paris, and become a poet.

(4) You strut your way into the ball. Devils and angels, harlequins and harlots, beasts and beauties, drink and dance in the ornate ballroom. A Count may be disguised as a humble fool, a woman of ill repute concealed in a nun's habit. The debauched atmosphere engulfs you, but you must stay true to your task. Your social rival Lady Eastaughffe will also try to secure the most eligible Earl's hand tonight. How will you sabotage her?

You drip the urine of a scullery maid on her dress. **(12)**
You spread a rumor Lady Eastaughffe has syphilis. **(13)**
Be the bigger person and do nothing. **(14)**

(11) You have a quiet life with the cemetery keeper. He is a simple man and never asks more of you than you are willing to give. Forty years and three children later, you are buried in the same grave he found you in all those years ago.

(12) Ingenious! When Lady Eastaughffe approaches the Earl, he is repulsed by the smell of poverty on her dress.

Acquire your celebratory glass of wine. **(6)**

(13) As you spread the rumor, it twists and everyone thinks you have "The French Disease." You have no hope for marriage and must join a convent.

(14) You take the high road. While you are congratulating yourself on your morality, Lady Eastaughffe tells everyone your dress is from last season. You are the laughingstock of the party. The next day you are engaged to the loathsome Baron Mortimer.

(6) Delicious! As you sip your wine, you watch couples dancing. A man in a harlequin mask asks you to dance. Beware false Earls. Lesser men love masquerade balls to propose to unsuspecting women, hoping they can nab a lady of a higher title. You...

Say yes **(15)**
Say no **(16)**

❖ ❖ ❖

(15) You share a waltz with the man, unsure of his identity. You must test him to see if he truly is the Earl of Collinwood. You...

Ask him about his time in the war. (17)
Ask him about his time in Italy. (18)
Ask him about his timepiece. (19)

❖ ❖ ❖

(16) The man in the harlequin mask melts into the crowd. You overhear a rumor that the Earl is wearing the mask of a Greek God. You see two Greek Gods on either side of the ballroom. You approach...

Zeus (20)
Hades (21)

❖ ❖ ❖

(17) The man regales you with stories of his brave actions. This does nothing to distinguish him, as every man believes himself a war hero. You...

Ask him about his time in Italy. (18)
Ask him about his timepiece. (19)

❖ ❖ ❖

(18) The man in the harlequin mask says he has never been to Italy. You know the Earl spent his summers in Rome. You abandon him after the dance is over. You search for the Earl in...

The library (22)

The balcony **(23)**

(20) As you approach the King of Gods, he smiles and puts an all too familiar arm around you. Zeus is Baron Mortimer in disguise. He tells everyone of your impending engagement, scaring away any other suitors.

(19) The man in the harlequin mask gets angry, saying women should not be thinking about such scientific things as the passage of time. He abandons you mid-waltz. Humiliated, you run away to the...

The library **(22)**
The balcony **(23)**

(21) As you approach the King of the Underworld, you recognize this god has the signature golden tooth of your friend Viscount Tewksbury. Relieved to find an ally among the revelers, you tell him of your plan. The Viscount believes he saw the Earl of Collinwood near the balcony. You...

Ignore his advice and go to the library. **(22)**
Follow his advice and go to the balcony. **(23)**

(22) In the library you find Lady Eastaughffe in a passionate embrace with one of Lady Worthingham's maids. You...

Back out quietly and go to the balcony. **(23)**
Confront them. **(24)**

◆ ◆ ◆

(23) As you walk toward the door to the balcony, you spy a handsome golden ram following you across the ballroom. As you exit into the chilly October evening, he follows. The man in the ram's mask remarks what a charming masquerade it has been. You say...

Yes. I do love a masquerade ball. **(25)**
No. I find the whole affair quite distasteful. **(26)**
What is your opinion of Carl Linnaeus's new system of binomial nomenclature for classifying animal life? **(27)**

(24) You clear your throat, interrupting the kissing pair. Lady Eastaughffe is mortified. She draws a blade from under her skirt and slices the throat of the maid then stabs herself in the breast. You are found with the dead bodies and arrested. Though you are found innocent, your experience has changed you. You no longer care for money or status, devoting yourself instead to the betterment of the conditions of English prisons. A life of charity assuages your guilt at confronting Lady East-aughffe, but every time you close your eyes you see her bleeding on the library rug.

◆ ◆ ◆

(25) I do as well, replies the golden ram. Isn't it wonderful? You reply...

Yes. I do love a masquerade ball. **(25)**
Are you the Earl of Collinwood? **(28)**

(27) "Um, sorry?" replies the Earl. He is a kind man, not a smart one. You say...

> Never mind. Will you marry me? **(31)**
> I cannot marry a man who does not have a firm grasp of the natural sciences. **(36)**

(28) "You have found me out," says the Earl, "And who are you?" You...

> Remove your mask. **(29)**
> Refuse to reveal your identity. **(30)**

(26) "Oh, that's too bad," says the ram, "Is there anything I could do to improve your spirits?" You say...

> Yes. Propose to me. **(31)**
> No. I am sure nothing will improve my mood. **(32)**

(29) As you untie your mask, one of Lady Worthingham's servants spots you from the ballroom. He rushes over and drags you out of the party for violating the strict no mask removal policy. You cannot return to the ball and the next day your father announces your engagement to Baron Mortimer.

(30) You shake your head, having read the fine print of the invitation regarding the strict no mask removal policy. The Earl of Collinwood loves a lady who strictly adheres to the instructions on an invitation. He proposes on the spot. You live a happy life and inherit your portion of your father's massive estate.

◆ ◆ ◆

(32) "Not even this?" The ram pulls out a beautiful amethyst and diamond ring and slips it on to your finger. "As I am the Earl of Collinwood, you shall be my wife. What shall I call you?" You say...

Earless of Collinwood **(33)**
Countess of Collinwood **(34)**
Duchess of Collinwood **(35)**

(31) The Earl is stunned by your forthrightness. He takes a step back, trips on a misplaced plumed hat, and tumbles off the balcony. His mask slips off as he falls, and you see the last look of terror in the eyes of your beloved Earl of Collinwood before he is impaled on the arm of a cherub on Lady Worthingham's fountain. You flee the ball and return home, shaken by what you have witnessed. A husk of your former self, you agree to the engagement to Baron Mortimer. Once you have given the Baron two sons, he ships you away to a lodge in the Swiss Alps for broken women, where you spend the rest of your hollow life.

(33) WRONG! The Earl removes the ring from your finger in disgust. He leaves you alone on the balcony, doomed to marry the detestable Baron Mortimer.

◆ ◆ ◆

(34) "Very well, Countess," the Earl says, pleased you know the feminine form of Earl is Countess. You marry your beloved Earl and live the rest of your life in comfort and happiness.

◆ ◆ ◆

(35) WRONG! The Earl removes the ring from your finger in disgust. He pushes you off the balcony. You fall to your death, cursing the fact you didn't pay closer attention when memorizing peerage titles.

◆ ◆ ◆

(36) You leave the ball and return home. You marry Baron Mortimer, produce a son, then kill the Baron with Hemlock in his evening port. Your young son inherits the estate and you embark on a globetrotting adventure, observing the wonders of the natural world.

Here's The Cemetery Where Every Man In Our Family Is Buried Alive

Hey sport, I have something to show you. This is our family's cemetery plot. It's where every member of the Milton clan is laid to rest. Remember Great Uncle Adam's funeral last summer? Here he is. And Grandpa Tommy? Right under that oak tree. And buddy, someday you're going to bury me here. Then way in the future, you'll be buried here. Because we bury every man in the Milton family here. One hundred percent alive.

Lots of families have traditions, li'l buddy. The Del Toros put on a live nativity at Christmas. Or the Costellos use their great-grandma's quilt for new babies. The Miltons toss every male member of our family alive into the Earth. No biggie. Don't cry, Cole. This is the natural circle of life. It's even on our family crest, the baby being born into a grave.

See, it all started in 1648. Augustus Milton was taking a nap on the floor of his study. His wife saw him there, thought he had died, and called for the doctor, the priest, and the undertaker. When the men arrived, they realized Augustus was asleep. Augustus was so embarrassed, he insisted on carrying on with the entire process so as not to waste anyone's time. Through everything, the funeral, the wake, the burial, Augustus was stoic. Everyone knew the great sacrifice he was making to save the family's honor, so from that day forward, every Milton accepts their live burial with grace.

How do we decide when? Sometimes everyone knows, like when Uncle Andy couldn't control his bowels anymore. But sometimes, there's dishonor in the family and to make up for it, we choose a man to bury.

Sure, Milton men have died before we could bury them alive. My cousin Stewart was hit by a drunk driver. He was buried somewhere, I guess, but not here on Milton land. A Milton man is buried alive

Women? As if women would go along with this hundred years old honor tradition. Milton women die as God intended, usually from breast cancer.

I bet you're wondering why I'm telling you this now. Ever since your Uncle Paul was indicted for tax evasion, the Milton name needs some honor. So this morning, the men got together over coffee and Danish to throw a dart at the old family tree. And son, the dart landed on me. With the legal fees from Uncle Paul, we can't afford a funeral so I came up here last night and dug my own grave. I just need you to finish the job.

Let me get on in. There should be a shovel up there near the pile of dirt. Son, grab the shovel and start burying. Be a man and bury your father alive. Cole, I swear to god if you mess this up like you did your last T-Ball game. Come on you little... woah, ok there we go. No need to call me names while you bury. Ugh ach, really aiming for the face now. Every animal instinct is telling me to get out of this grave and live, but I'm sure this is what every Milton man since Augustus has felt. The sting of betrayal and pride as your own flesh and blood buries you alive.

You're the man of the house now, Cole. Tell mom I said to take you to Cold Stone and you can order whatever you want. Also, I love her too, I guess.

I should say my last words. A Milton man's last words are really something because he knows he's about to die. Ok, the meaning of life is... ahh, there's a worm in my mouth. No those can't be my last...

A Plea To The Stranger Sending Me Cardboard Boxes Of Baked Beans

Dear Mysterious Bean Stranger,

Eight months ago I arrived home from work to find an 18x18 cardboard box on the front porch of my condo. Assuming it was the four-pack of throw pillows I had ordered; I nudged the box toward my front door with my foot. Instead of scooting the box into my foyer, my foot pierced the swollen cardboard and a spout of baked beans burst through the puncture. Sticky, sugary, smoky beans flooded my porch, ruining my white sneakers and glooping all over my azaleas.

I hosed off the porch and threw the box in the trash, assuming I was the victim of a prank. Until a week later, when the second box arrived. This one I examined more closely. A standard cardboard shipping box with the word Beans scrawled on the side in Sharpie. I ripped off the tape and found the contents to be as advertised.

At first, it was a nightmare. Three or four times a week, gushing boxes of creamy beans spilling over my porch. I come home from work: Beans. I go outside to get the mail: Beans. I go for a thirty-minute run and come back to find a sodden box of: Beans. Neighbors complained about the smell of liquid smoke and swarms of ants. I contacted the post office, FedEx, UPS, but no one was delivering the beans.

Who would do this? A friend thought it might be a vengeful ex-boyfriend. A co-worker suggested it was a poorly executed Van Camp's marketing stunt. After frantic Google searches ("beans boxes" "bean curses" "cardboard box of beans on porch WHY") I saw no one else had reported this phenomenon.

The logistics terrified me. Were you cooking vast quantities of beans to torment me? Or were these canned beans purchased in bulk and emptied into the boxes? Were the boxes transported with the beans inside, or were you filling the box on my porch? And why me? Had I summoned the beans? Why was I, a normal thirty-seven-year-old paralegal, chosen? Why me?

After I posted on Facebook about the phenomenon, a local reporter asked to write a story. Did you read it? Is that why the beans escalated? Did you enjoy the attention? The reporter set up a motion-sensitive camera on my front porch, but it caught no footage. When the reporter opened it to check the SD card, the inside of the camera was replaced with beans.

I became a local celebrity. Every evening, kids would swarm my porch. I would slice open the side of the box with a knife, beans gushing forth like blood from a carotid artery. But instead of horror, children shrieked in delight as I soaked them in warm beans. They even invited me on The Today Show, sharing my tale with millions of Americans in waiting rooms. Duke, The Bush's Baked Beans Dog, followed me on Twitter.

And then you stopped.

Days, then weeks passed with no boxes of beans arriving at my door. Had I displeased you? Or had my time in the maple hickory spotlight come to its natural end? Every evening I came home from work expecting to see a seeping cardboard box on my porch and every evening I was disappointed. The kids stopped coming around. Even the ants left, drawn to my neighbor's unsealed compost bin.

I thought quitting smoking was the hardest thing I would ever do. At least with cigarettes, I could go back whenever I wanted. But I couldn't replace the beans. I ordered thirty cans of Bush's Bold & Spicy Baked Beans online. When they arrived, I opened the cans and poured them into the box they came in. It was not the same. Gifts are never as good when you give them to yourself.

At three in the morning, I sleepwalked through the aisles

of my local Kroger. I stood in the bean aisle taking can after can off the shelves, stabbing them with my pocket knife, and letting them ooze onto the linoleum. The manager shook me awake.

"Hey, you can't do that," he said, then he recognized me, "I saw you on the Today Show in my podiatrist's office. You're that bean lady."

I shook my head and moaned in sorrow.

"What are you doing here? Don't you have beans at home?"

"I did, I did. But I didn't savor them. I thought the beans would never stop." I glugged half a can of Kroger Brand Home-style Baked Beans, choking on the glob of fat at the bottom of the can.

"Oh, that must be a relief, not having to deal with those beans all the time."

I handed him a fifty-dollar bill and left the store. It's not a relief to be average. Not when you've tasted the maple hickory nectar of being chosen.

Please Bean Stranger. I need these boxes of sweet and smoky validation to keep going. Last night I poured a hundred cans of baked beans into my bathtub. I hid my naked form in the basin of beans, sinking into the sugary swill, eating, weeping, and giving myself a nasty yeast infection.

I'm running this ad in every major newspaper, hoping you see it and keep sending the boxes. I promise I won't waste my second chance. I won't waste a single bean.

Forever Yours,
The (Former) Bean Queen

News From The Front

"A letter from Sam? Is it news from the front?" Tottie leaned over her older sister's shoulder to peek at the piece of paper in her hand.

"It's a tragedy." Delia threw the letter across her bedroom into a dusty corner. Both girls cleaned other people's homes all day and had no energy to spruce up their own filthy hovel.

Tottie scanned the letter. It was the usual sweetheart wishes, complaints about the trenches, and promises he would be back in Peterborough as soon as God would allow. Sam the fishmonger's son and Delia the washerwoman's daughter weren't exactly Romeo and Juliet, but Tottie tolerated her sister's hysteria over her fiancé fighting on the western front. Last week Tottie had thought she'd left her favorite gloves at church, so she knew what it was to fear a terrible loss.

"War hasn't improved his spelling," said Tottie, "but I don't see why you're so faint over a boring old love letter from Gallipoli."

"Read the postscript," said Delia, flinging herself onto her bed like an overdramatic swan.

"P.S. Another fella keeps a lock of his wife's hair in his pocket and I'd love to have a piece of yours to keep with me." Tottie burst out laughing.

Delia screeched as she pawed at her freshly shaved head. "I thought that by the time he returned it would have grown back." Delia pointed an accusing finger at her bald little sister. "This is all your fault."

"Me?" Tottie scrambled behind a chair, out of her sister's angry grasp. "It weren't me who brought the buggers into the house. I bet it was Blousy."

Delia lunged at Tottie, who scampered into a corner using

Sam's letter as a shield.

"And it's you," screeched Delia, "who insists on letting that damned nit infested cat sleep in our bed." She jumped at Tottie but overshot, banging her head on the wall, and crumpling into a weeping ball against the doorframe. "What am I going to do? Sam will never marry a hairless monster."

"Hey," said Tottie, putting her arms around her sobbing sister, "Of course, Sam will marry you. He knows Pa will wring his neck if he doesn't make you an honest woman after Pa caught you two naked..."

"Shut it."

"Get a lock of hair from Mary Duggins. Sam won't know the difference." Mary's brown waves were a perfect match for Delia's former locks.

"But I will know the difference. What if he... if he dies out there clutching a lock of another woman's hair? Tottie, I couldn't live with myself if I let him cling on to a lie."

Tottie grinned. "Luckily, we didn't shave you everywhere."

Rocky Road

The Gravel Salesman was out of options. He'd promised his boss at Honey River Stone & Gravel he could sell three thousand tons of quarter inch pea gravel by the end of the month. He'd smacked his palm on DeWayne's desk as if throwing down a gauntlet.

"I'll sell it all and if I don't, I want you to fire me. No, I want you to ruin me. If I don't sell this gravel by August first, you can send my wife that picture from the Christmas party of me getting busy with Harvey's wife in the copy room. Hell, put it on the internet along with my name and address."

Why, oh, why had he constructed this impossible challenge? Was it shame at getting outsold the previous month by the new saleswoman, Mattie? A ploy to humiliate his new boss, DeWayne, who he was sure had been promoted to fill a racial quota? Or a challenge to himself, to prove he was still worth something in a world no longer impressed by him for simply existing?

In the good old days it had been so easy. When his Grandpa had co-founded Honey River Stone & Gravel, all a man needed was a shovel and a firm handshake and he could sell gravel to anyone. Growing up, the Gravel Salesman had watched his father make three deals before lunch all by calling his Elks buddies who needed new driveways. Then he'd spend the rest of the afternoon getting drunk on the porch. That was a real man.

And now, the Gravel Salesman had the lowest sales numbers at the company started by his own Pawpaw. It was humiliating to be bossed around by these diversity hires. Sure, put them in the middle of the frame in the company photo, but you weren't actually supposed to put them at the center of your company.

After twenty-eight days of calling in favors, dialing up

random people from the phone book, and begging family members to re-gravel their walkways, he was still a thousand tons short of his goal. He knew DeWayne was looking for an excuse to fire him and a compromising photo was the perfect ammunition. The Gravel Salesman also worried about his wife finding out. The cow eyed creature with whom he shared a bed might forgive late nights and suspicious VISA charges, but a picture would be a wound no box of chocolate meringues could heal.

His last hope had come in the form of his eleven-year-old daughter, Penelope. The Gravel Salesman had wanted kids until the moment he held her in his arms. He'd almost dropped her, stunned by how heavy she was. A toothless black hole. His wife had wanted another, and the Gravel Salesman thought a son might be different, but he couldn't take the chance of getting another dead weight, so he got a vasectomy. All he knew about his daughter was that she loved horses, asked for chicken nuggets for every meal, and from the many interminable school plays he'd sat through, he knew she had a knack for memorizing lines.

When the Gravel Salesman had asked Penelope if she could memorize lines and deliver them for him, she was shocked. For years, she had begged her father to help her practice her lines. From Marian in Jardine Middle School's spring production of *The Music Man* to Martha Cratchit in Jardine Middle School's winter production of *A Christmas Carol*, Penelope had pleaded for her father to take notice of her passion for the stage. And now, he'd written a script just for her? Maybe Johanna, her coach at Christian soccer camp, had been right about the power of patience.

Sunday morning they'd drilled the script in the living room. The Gravel Salesman's wife was at work, taking an extra shift at the nursing home to save up for a new transmission for her Camry. His wife would have scolded him for making his daughter a prop in his sales scheme. But he'd made Penelope swear she wouldn't tell her mom.

"We have a secret? Just us?" Her heart swelled with her

father's trust. "Let's pinky swear." She looped her finger around the Gravel Salesman's pinky then kissed her thumb.

"Okay," he said, extricating his hand from his daughter's sweaty grip, "How quick can you get these lines memorized?"

Over and over, Penelope recited her lines, the Gravel Salesman noting where her smile looked fake or her delivery unnatural. He even had her improvise a few lines in case they had to go off script. Penelope lapped up even his harshest criticism, determined to prove to him she was a child star in the making. Even the most difficult part, the eating, she had agreed to without hesitation.

He had eschewed larger ice cream chains, the Cold Stone Creamery, the Baskin Robbins, because of their tall corporate ladders. This idea had to sell fast. He needed access to the man in charge today. So after a Google search, he landed on Spoons Creamery, which had three locations in the greater Kansas City area. It sold gourmet flavors that included flower petals and sea salt. Perfect. Liberal try-anything hipsters would eat this idea up.

They dressed in their Christmas church clothes, digging them out from the back of their spare closet. The Gravel Salesman in a navy blue suit and matching trilby and Penelope in an itchy red velvet dress with an enormous bow plastered on top of her head. She'd grown out of the matching Mary Janes, so she put on her favorite rainbow Keds. Together they looked like a 50s G-Man and a rich orphan who witnessed her mother's murder.

The entire drive over Penelope recited her lines in the backseat of the gray Nissan, her stomach rumbling because the Gravel Salesman had insisted she skip lunch so she wouldn't have to act hungry. As he parked in front of the strip mall containing Spoons Creamery, he exhaled, sure his plan was about to save him. It might do even more than save him. If he could convince this company of his idea, who knew how far he could go. He imagined a phone call with Ben & Jerry, congratulating him on his innovation and asking where to send the check.

He held Penelope's hand as they entered the modern space. A large glass case of ice creams to the left, an empty seating area of orange tables to the right. Blue wallpaper with a pattern of silver spoons adorned the walls along with a signed headshot of Annette Bening. A blasé teen scooper with three piercings in each ear stood behind the case, a smear of chocolate on their orange apron.

"Welcome to Spoons Creamery, the Creamiest Place on Earth," said the scooper, putting on a service industry smile. "What can I scoop you up today?"

"Wow, lavender rose ice cream. I don't know, Penelope. This place seems pretty innovative. Are you sure you'll find something you like?" The Gravel Salesman took an exaggerated step back toward the door.

"Of course, silly Daddy. I love to try new ice cream trends." Penelope stamped her Keds and pointed her finger in the air. "In fact, even more than most kids my age, I'd say I know a good trend that will increase a business's profits for sure."

"Wow, Penelope. You're a kid with a pulse on the trends of tomorrow."

The bored scooper steeled themselves for whatever sect of Christianity the man and his daughter were going to pitch. Wackadoos periodically came in to convert customers and give tips of fake hundred-dollar bills with apocalyptic Bible verses on the back. The scooper wished they were someplace more pleasant, like the nine hundred degree surface of Venus.

The Gravel Salesman stepped up to the counter, while Penelope pretended to browse the various flavors. "I'll try a sample of your Maple Brown Butter Blueberry."

The scooper handed the Gravel Salesman a small wooden spoon with a dollop of beige ice cream.

"Yum yum," said the Gravel Salesman. He could tell this teenaged scooper wasn't the man in charge, but he was sure if he played it right, he'd be on the phone to the big boss in no time. "This place is a hip joint on the cutting edge. Not afraid to try something out of the box. What flavor do you want to try, honey?"

"What's in Rocky Road?" asked Penelope, making her eyes big and innocent. She pointed to the small plastic sign on the glass case.

"It's our premium milk chocolate ice cream with home-made marshmallow swirl, hickory infused caramel, and black walnuts." The scooper pitied the girl. She kept glancing at her father as if he were a pot that at any moment might boil over with praise. "Do you want a sample?"

"Yes please." Penelope stuck out her hungry tongue and rubbed her belly.

The scooper handed a wooden spoon of rocky road to the girl. The Gravel Salesman pretended to be deciding between Macadamia Mint and Caramel Pumpkin Curry but was listening for his cue.

Penelope slurped the tiny scoop and spit the ice cream onto the ground. She rubbed her tongue on her velvet sleeve.

"What's the matter?" asked the Gravel Salesman.

"I just gave her a sample of the Rocky Road," said the star-tled scooper. They felt the same way they had at their cousin's Amway-themed birthday party. They were being sold some-thing, but they weren't sure what.

"It's not good, Daddy. The Rocky Road isn't good at all." Penelope tried to squeeze out a few tears to sell her disappoint-ment. "It doesn't have any rocks in it!"

"No rocks? Why, that's false advertising!" The Gravel Salesman pointed at the plastic sign. "There it is, plain as day, Rocky Road. It's like selling Cookies & Cream without cookies. Or Butter Pecan with no nuts."

The scooper sighed. The man must not be a religious freak, but a litigious freak. "If you're trying to start a lawsuit…"

"Lawsuit? Lawsuit!" cried the Gravel Salesman, throwing his hands in the air.

"Lawsuit! Lawsuit?" echoed Penelope, putting her hands up as well.

"I'm trying to save you from a lawsuit, young man." The

Gravel Salesman took off his trilby and placed it over his heart. He looked sincerely at the scooper, the same look he reserved for solemn things such as funerals and the American flag.

The scooper was non-binary, but if there was a time to let a misgendering slide, it was now. "Listen, I can offer you two free scoops. Any flavor you want." Offering something for free. The service worker's panacea.

"Daddy, Daddy, I want Rocky Road with actual rocks." Penelope felt so confident delivering her big line, she stood on an orange chair. "It's a surefire trend that's going to explode within the next three to four months. I want to be on the leading edge of this culinary sensation about to sweep the ice cream nation."

"It's a cutting edge trend and will save Spoons Creamery from potential future lawsuits? That's what I call a win-win!" The Gravel Salesman had never before been proud of his daughter.

"But Daddy, how will this premium ice cream shop gain access to enough premium rocks to take advantage of this premium opportunity? Wouldn't they need at least a thousand tons of premium quarter inch pea gravel at a wholesale price?"

"You're right, daughter of mine, but I don't think this guy believes Rocky Road with rocks is the taste sensation that will prevent lawsuits we say." The Gravel Salesman winked at the unconvinced scooper. He worried he'd put too many ideas into the script. Should he have just focused on the lawsuit? Picked a lane? Too late now. "My daughter will have one scoop of Rocky Road in a waffle bowl, please."

Penelope clambered down from the chair. The scooper retrieved a waffle bowl, put a scoop of Rocky Road inside, and handed it to Penelope. To their horror, the father and daughter sat at a table to continue this demented charade.

As she placed the bowl of ice cream in front of her, Penelope got a rare chill. The same chill when she hit the high notes in *Till There Was You* during Jardine Middle School's spring production of *The Music Man*. The chill of a job well done. Now, onto the second act.

The Gravel Salesman joined her at the table and took a bite of her ice cream. "Ew. You're right, honey, this could use some rocks." He took a plastic baggie of gravel from his breast pocket and dumped it into the bowl, dust and silt flying over the orange tabletop. The gravel engulfed the ice cream. "Now try, sweet daughter of mine."

This was Penelope's big moment. If she didn't sell it right, it ruined the whole game. Her dad smiled, encouraging her to take a bite. In her spoon she scooped a smidge of chocolate ice cream covered in pebbles. Closing her eyes, she jammed the whole thing in her mouth. Rocks smashed into her teeth. The same pain she had felt pulling her last baby tooth out with a piece of floss, magnified by ten. The bitter grit of the stones eclipsed the flavor of chocolate. She bit down, trying to trick her throat into swallowing, and was pummeled by a wave of pain emanating from her right back molar. After ten excruciating swallows, the rocks were down her throat.

"Yummy yum yum, what a treat! I'd eat this every day and I know every kid in America will love it, just like me." She did a thumbs up and a cute little wink at the scooper, like she had seen a kid in a Cheerios commercial do.

The Gravel Salesman, watching his daughter struggle to swallow the gravel, decided to skip to the next part of the script. What a disappointment. He'd seen the girl gulp down half a large pizza in a minute flat, but when it really mattered she was sputtering and slobbering everywhere. She was supposed to finish the entire bowl, but he couldn't chance her choking and throwing off the whole sale. The specter of DeWayne laughing as he sent the picture to everyone in his contacts loomed before him. No, he would not let this be the end of him. Taken down by a kid who couldn't eat a bowl of ice cream.

He felt in his pocket for his wallet. He'd left it in his other pants. Damn, how was he supposed to seal the gravel deal with Scoops Creamery without his business card? It was the last line of the script. He would hand his card to the astonished and fully convinced scooper and say, "If you need gravel, I have a scoop on where you can buy some." Then he'd put on his hat and walk away like James Bond. But he couldn't do that without his card.

"I'll be back in a moment," the Gravel Salesman announced to the empty ice cream shop. He hurried out to search his car for a spare business card.

The scooper wanted no part in whatever this was. The girl in the velvet dress pretending to eat rocks (that were surely just candy) while her father yelled about lawsuits was too much for a Sunday afternoon. They were going to quit Spoons Creamery in a few weeks when they headed back to college, anyway. Why not leave now? Before the awful man could return, the scooper hung up their apron, grabbed their stuff from their locker, and sent a text to their coworker promising all the shrooms he could take if he covered the rest of their shift.

This wasn't part of the plan. Even in all the improvs they had done, Penelope's dad had never left her alone. Penelope had swallowed her first spoonful of gravel, but obviously that hadn't been enough. Her father was so disappointed in her lackluster acting he was abandoning the plan altogether. The scooper had disappeared. Probably to go laugh at what a terrible actress Penelope was. That she couldn't get right the one role that counted. She mashed the gravel into the ice cream, trying to make an easier-to-choke-down slurry, and gulped another bite.

In the script, it had said for her to finish the whole bowl, pat her tummy and say, "I'd eat this Rocky Road for breakfast, lunch, and dinner. That's the truth!" Her dad was still in the car. Maybe if he saw she'd finished the whole bowl he'd come back.

Another tooth zinged with pain. Penelope dug the plastic spoon into her rocky Rocky Road and jammed in another bite. It might hurt but a good actress knew to never question her director. She could see it now, her dad coming into the ice cream shop with pride in his eyes at the good job his little girl had done.

As the Gravel Salesman searched his glove compartment for a business card, his phone buzzed. It was a text from his buddy that the Lake Shawnee golf course was re-graveling their walkways. Shit, if he could get a handshake on this by the end of the day, he'd win. He'd be the month's top seller and DeWayne wouldn't post the picture. This was how it was supposed to work. A call from a buddy leading to a deal over a cold beer.

As he backed out of the parking spot and sped toward the golf course, he cranked up the radio and sang along. He'd show them he wasn't washed up, wasn't second rate. He got where he got through hard work and nothing but. Tonight, when he came home, he'd be able to make love to his wife, safe in the fact a tiny indiscretion wouldn't rock his marriage. It was going to be alright.

The scooper leaned against the outside of the employee entrance, waiting for their replacement to show up. They saw the Gravel Salesman's gray Nissan leaving the parking lot and assumed the father and daughter had given up their wild scene. They texted their coworker, *never mind.* Without the loonies, the scooper could have a normal Sunday shift.

They went back inside and put on their apron. The man was gone, but the girl lay slumped on the table, spoon dropped to the floor, the bowl completely empty.

An Advice Column Written By Someone In The Witness Protection Program

Dear ████████████,

Even after twenty years of marriage, I still get annoyed when my husband won't put his socks in the hamper, put a dirty dish in the dishwasher, or take out the trash when it's full. He's a great husband otherwise, but these little things are driving me nuts. How can I get over it?

Sincerely,

Frustrated Wife

Dear Frustrated,

When I was married in ████████████ my wife would ████████. Even when I asked her to ████████████ she would still ████████. Later, when I found myself ████████ the ████ for the ████████, I missed even the things about her that annoyed me. Treasure your husband and know there's something you do that annoys him just as much.

Best,

████████████

❖ ❖ ❖

Dear ████████████,

I'm in a very delicate situation. I've made some wrong choices in life, but none as bad as my friend K. K is a liar and a cheater but everyone believes he's a good guy. I feel like if I tell people who the real K is, everyone will turn against me. I'll have to leave town and start over somewhere else. Should I take the risk and expose K or keep my mouth shut?

Thanks,

Conflicted in OKC

Dear Conflicted,

I know it might feel like a betrayal, but you've got to tell everyone about K! Seriously, you'll feel better and starting a new life isn't so bad. When I was living in ████████, I testified ███████████████████████. Now I'm a very happy advice columnist living in ████████with ███████████████████████ ██████

Good luck,

████████████

◆ ◆ ◆

Dear ████████████

I'm a manager at a Fortune 500 company. Last week was take your daughter to work day so I brought my ten-year-old daughter Amelia to work with me. Everyone thought it was cute that a ten-year-old was trying to follow along with our quarterly meeting. That is, until she corrected my projections for third-quarter earnings. I told her to be quiet until Dale checked her math and found out she was right. It was embarrassing, but I managed to laugh it off. Then she was in my office as I had a conference call with a client from Beijing. Amelia looked up from her Nintendo and started talking to the client in perfect Mandarin. I had no idea what they were saying, but judging by how much the client was laughing, I think a lot of it was about me. She also got them to double their orders and they invited her to visit their offices in Beijing the next time she's in town. I was getting frustrated with Amelia by this point so I told her to go grab us some granola bars from the break room so I could cool off. But of course, she runs into the CEO who is also grabbing a snack. I don't know what she said to him, but pretty soon they're having a closed-door meeting, while I wondered what I was going to tell her mother. Long story short, my ten-year-old daughter is now my boss. I'm very proud of her, but it's hard to drive my daughter to the office every day, drop her off at the executive suite, then go down to my windowless office. And discipline is a nightmare. You try telling your CFO that she has to brush her teeth every night and can't say the f-word even though everyone else in the C-suite does. Do I need to find a new job?

Best,
Worried Dad

Dear Worried,
Wow, what a pickle! I'd advise you ███████████████ ███████████████████████████. Even though ██████████ ██ and ███████████████████████████████████ ████████████████████████████████ My most import-ant insight would be to ███████████████████████ ██Do this and you'll be sure to be sharing the C-Suite soon.
Good luck!
Sincerely,
█████████

◆ ◆ ◆

Dear ███████████,
My dad puts sprinkles on everything he eats. It's so em-barrassing to eat anywhere with him and I'm worried about his health, both dental and mental.
Thanks,
Son of Sprinkles

Dear SOS,

In situations like these my grandma ███████ used to say, ███ ██████████████████████████████████. Growing up in ██████ in the ████ she faced a lot of hardship and I think those wise words perfectly apply to your situation. If all else fails ███████████████████████████████████████ ██████████

Good luck,

██████████

A Single Walgreen's Rose

Seven pm on February 14th you hurry into the Walgreens a mile from your house desperate for a physical manifestation of the feeling society tells you is love. Your wife of six years, Bianca, has prepared coq au vin because you forgot to make a reservation at that Italian place she likes. You scurry through the aisles of the Walgreens frantically picking up items. A white teddy bear holding a felt heart, a box of chocolate-covered pretzel rods, a bottle of the fruit-shaped gummy vitamins she takes that are 50% off. You grab a red gift bag. It features Santa and his reindeer, but eh, close enough. You're an hour late because you stayed at work playing ping pong with the engineers. For nerds, those guys are pretty fun.

Winded, you arrive in line to check out. Your eyes scan the impulse buys. As you grab a tin of Altoids, you see me, standing in a bucket among my brothers. A de-thorned red rose in a thin plastic sleeve. I'm $5.99. My petals are cracking at the edges. Bianca likes flowers, right? No time to think. You slam me on the counter, type in the phone number connected to your Walgreens rewards account, and jam your Amex into the chip reader.

Driving like a maniac, you blow past the stop sign Bianca started the petition to make the city install. You pull into your driveway, sprint up the stairs, and burst into your condo screaming, "Happy Valentine's Day." The kitchen smells of chicken and chocolate and you find Bianca icing a red velvet cake, a half-eaten plate of coq au vin on the island next to her.

God, she's beautiful. Even wearing that dress you hate because it makes her breasts look like one long blue silk rectangle, she's so much hotter than you. I know I'm simply a rapidly decaying long-stemmed Floribunda, but you two have the attractiveness differential of a couple in a 90s sitcom.

"I got hungry," she says as you present her with the bag of gifts.

Her eyebrows raise at the jolly Santa on the bag, but she says nothing. She smiles at the fuzzy bear, before ripping the price tag off his ear. She takes out a pretzel rod and snaps it between her teeth like a hyena with the leg of a gazelle. She places the vitamins in the cabinet, nodding at their practicality. Then she gets to me. The solitary rose. A flicker of a smile at the whisper of a romantic gesture.

"Happy Valentine's Day," you whisper, hoping this is enough. That this plastic bag of garbage will buy you a few more months of affection. Her birthday is in June. You promise yourself you'll make a reservation at that new Vietnamese place she wants to try, and get her an enormous basket of those overpriced bath bombs she enjoys.

You won't.

She digs through a cabinet for a vase. As she fills the vase with water, you unwrap me from my sad plastic sheath. She sets the half-filled vase on the counter and you place me into the water. I thunk to the side, unable to hold myself up. If I had peers, eleven more brothers and sisters I could stand, but I swoon under the weight of my own flower. Bianca touches a velvet petal and it floats to the linoleum.

"I made you a plate." Out of the oven comes a warm plate of coq au vin, caramelized Brussels sprouts, and a fluffy yeast roll. You exhale, remove your jacket, and sit at the island to enjoy your meal.

She picks up her spatula and continues icing the red velvet cake. While you're eating, I watch Bianca spreading the cream cheese icing, piping pink florets around the bottom edge, arranging chalky sugar letters to say "Happy Valentine's Day" on the top. Bianca looks like a fun dental hygienist. One who talks a little shit about how the dentist is wearing a skull cap to hide his bald spot to help calm patients' nerves.

"This chicken is amazing. Is this the one from Whole

Foods?" You chew the last of your coq and slurp up the vin.

"Uh-huh, the organic one. You want some cake?" She snaps a few pictures for Instagram, then cuts you each a thick slice.

You eat in silence, moving bits of sweet red cake from plate to mouth, plate to mouth, until you can't take the silence anymore. "Alexa, play Beyonce," you shout into the living room.

Bianca bobs her head as she picks up a chocolate covered pretzel rod and dunks it in her extra cream cheese frosting. "I was out of those vitamins."

"Really?"

"Took the last one this morning."

I am suffocating. Neither of you snipped the dry end of my stem. Water water everywhere, but not a drop to drink.

"Maybe," she says, "maybe we could start trying. It took my sister a whole year, so if we start now, by the time it happens we'll be…"

You kiss her before she can finish the thought. For an awkward moment, you try to boost her onto the counter, but you aren't strong enough, so you pull her upstairs to your bedroom. You'll make love on top of your Pottery Barn duvet under the mis-attributed inspirational quote hanging on the wall.

I could let go now. Let my essence fade into the ether of your pale blue kitchen. But I hold on. I wonder what Bianca was going to say? When you'll be… financially stable? Ready? Older? Wiser? Happy?

All I know is that in nine months you'll be scrambling down the aisles of another Walgreens. Past 70% off Halloween decorations and a display of hard seltzers, trying to find a knick-knack for a woman with her cervix dilated six inches.

And I'm just a rose that's been sitting in a plastic bin next to a cash register for a week, so I don't have a fully formed conception of what happens after death. But I like to think you'll find me again. Your sweaty fingers will grab a plastic case of foiled wrapped Ferrero Rocher, a tube of mascara, and a sequined Beanie Baby sloth named Dangler.

You'll wait behind a woman arguing about her expired coupon and your eyes will find the tub of roses, dyed black and orange for Halloween, almost dead, and $1.78 each. You grab me and buy me and bring me to the hospital with you. And you bring me along to your wife, laying out what you have hunted for her. Showing her your worth.

God Pitches Ideas To Gabriel

God approaches Gabriel, who is relaxing on a cloud.

God: So I had a thought.

Gabriel: Uh-huh.

God: What if humans had a place that was half inside and half outside? A tiny platform jutting out from their homes?

Gabriel: Don't humans die if they fall from over twenty feet?

God: I'll give them a railing. But don't you think they'll enjoy it? Stepping onto their outside platform on a summer night to look at the stars.

Gabriel: So it's a seasonal thing?

God: Well yeah, I guess you could go out there in the winter if you needed a smoke.

Gabriel: Seems dangerous. Can't humans just go outside and stay on the ground?

God: I'm telling you; this is a good idea.

Gabriel sinks into the cloud, slowly disappearing.

God appears as a lamb during Gabriel's harp practice.

God: Women wear a lot of dresses, right?

Gabriel: You only recently made it acceptable for them to wear anything else.

God: Oversight on my end. Now, I want to even the score. What if dresses had pockets?

Gabriel: Won't that ruin the dress, though? If you have a wallet, keys, makeup, tampons, a pack of gum-

God: They wouldn't be able to put everything in there. But they could put like, a business card or a Starburst in there.

Gabriel: So they're still going to have to carry purses.

God: Well… probably.

Gabriel: Why have pockets in the first place? Isn't this an empty gesture after giving them the pain of childbirth and millennia of subservience to men?

God: You're wrong. Women are going to love this. They'll plunge their hands into those pockets and squeal, "It has pockets," every time someone compliments the dress. You'll see.

Gabriel sighs and turns up his electric harp.

God sidles up to Gabriel at the Heaven library, whispering in his ear.

God: So, humans are enjoying carnivals.

Gabriel: Yep, cotton candy and Ferris wheels are a big hit.

God: What if they could play games and win things? Something to remember the fun day at the carnival by?

Gabriel: Like a stuffed animal or miniature basketball?

God: Sure sure, but what if also a live fish?

Gabriel: Like a bass?

God: No, just a goldfish in a plastic sack. The humans throw balls into cups of water and if they hit a certain color, they get a fish.

Gabriel: Are the fish in the cups?

God: Let's say sometimes.

Gabriel: What are people supposed to do with it? Walk around the carnival for the rest of the day with a fish in a bag?

God: I mean, that's not such a burden.

Gabriel: And then it has to survive the hot car ride home.

God: It's in water, Gabriel.

Gabriel: And these people, who woke up that morning with no intention of getting a pet are plunged into goldfish ownership with no supplies or knowledge of fish care?

God: It's not rocket science.

Gabriel: Seems like a recipe for children to learn about their own fragile mortality after a fun day at the carnival. Is that what you were going for?

God: If I said yes, would you like the idea more?

Gabriel: Not really.

Gabriel dissipates into a sweet-smelling vapor.

God runs next to Gabriel as he plays Cloud Polo on a unicorn.

God: What if there were cameras recording animals? Like, you could sit in your own home and watch an eagle in her nest a thousand miles away.

Gabriel: To give humans empathy for all of your creations?

God: Mostly because they're cute, but empathy too, sure.

Gabriel scores a cloud polo goal.

God: Nice one. Also, I don't know if you heard, but balconies have been great. A few collapses in the beginning, but humans are really enjoying them.

Gabriel: If you're always right, and you are because you're *God*, why are you running these things by me?

God: Because we're friends and I value your opinion.

Gabriel stops his unicorn and looks into the face of God.

Gabriel: Oh, I didn't know that.

God: What? That we were friends or that I value you?

Gabriel: Both, I guess.

Gabriel resumes playing Cloud Polo, while God stands at the sideline, watching.

God's head appears in Gabriel's fireplace as he is napping on the couch.

God: BRUNCH!

Gabriel: What?

God: It's a new meal. Half breakfast, half lunch. It's mostly for weekends.

Gabriel: Why, though? You can eat breakfast or lunch anytime.

God: No, brunch is special. It's an event. You're not eating, you're brunching. It'll be served from ten to two. You can have anything from French toast to a BLT.

Gabriel: Okay, so it's an excuse to eat dinner food in the morning. I get to start my day with spaghetti?

God: No, spaghetti isn't brunch.

Gabriel: But I could have spaghetti for lunch.

God: Sure, but not brunch.

Gabriel: What about pork belly?

God: Brunch

Gabriel: Pork chops?

God: Not brunch.

Gabriel: Hash browns?

God: Yep.

Gabriel: Mashed potatoes?

God: Never.

Gabriel: A salad with raspberry vinaigrette.

God: Brunch it up.

Gabriel: A Caesar salad?

God: Go to Hell.

Gabriel: It's a lot of stress for a meal.

God: Everyone will love it. I'll give them bottomless mimosas to make sure.

Gabriel pretends to be asleep until God goes away.

Gabriel spills wine on his rug. God appears in the stain.

God: What if there were pills that make humans happy?

Gabriel: You already gave them MDMA. And then you made it illegal.

God: These pills wouldn't be illegal. And they wouldn't make you *that* happy. Just a normal amount.

Gabriel: Why would people take them?

God: If people are unhappy, they could take these pills and feel better. Antidepressants.

Gabriel: Ok, I like this idea, but since we're friends, may I throw out a suggestion?

God: By all means.

Gabriel: Maybe don't make them depressed?

God: But then what would antidepressants do?

Gabriel: I'm saying you wouldn't need them.

God: But if no one's depressed, where's the great art going to come from?

Gabriel: I'm pretty sure that's a myth.

God: It's not a myth if I started it.

Gabriel pours vinegar on the stain.

Gabriel is feeding ducks on a bench. God sits next to him.

God: Okay, hear me out, salted caramel.

Gabriel: Another food idea?

God: I'm not saying a lot of salt, just a pinch.

Gabriel: Why, though? Who wants to take a bite of flan and be like, ooh, salty?

God: The contrast makes it sweeter.

Gabriel: Whatever you say.

God: Fuck you, Gabriel. I'm going to make humans obsessed with combining salty and sweet. A pinch of sugar to pasta sauce. A sprinkle of salt on chocolate chip cookies. Dipping French fries in a milkshake. Those fucks will beg for two tastes at once.

Gabriel: Jeez, fine. Salty and sweet is a good idea.

Gabriel throws the last of the bread to the ducks and gets up to leave.

God: Sorry, I've been feeling inadequate lately. Everyone wants world peace or the end of female genital mutilation or a year-round McRib.

Gabriel: Two of those are good projects to focus on.

God: I thought if I worked on the small stuff, the big things would work themselves out. A broken windows theory of ruling over creation.

Gabriel: Did you read that Malcolm Gladwell book?

God: I love him. He makes science so accessible.

Gabriel: Because it's based on flawed data.

God: Shit, really? And the ten thousand hours thing?

Gabriel: Also wrong. Why don't you focus your creative energy on helping humans with big problems? Maybe racism? Or killings in your name? Or climate change?

God: But that's less fun. I'm tired of being a strict Old Testament God. Can't I just give them glow in the dark fingers?

Gabriel: For sex? No, don't distract me. The next idea you pitch me had better be genuinely helpful to humanity. No more 4-D movies or hyper-specific dating apps.

God: Feline acupuncturists need love too.

Gabriel starts to float away.

God: Climate change! I'll make it so humans travel less and they'll see how much the environment improves. It'll be a good lesson.

Gabriel: How will you make them travel less?

God: I don't know? A plague? They've worked in the past.

Gabriel: Um, maybe focus on the McRib.

Jobs That Would Make Terrible Premises For The Plot Of Porn

Slaughterhouse Worker
Roller Rink Disc Jockey
Funeral Home Director
Methane/Landfill Gas Generation System Technician
CDC Infection Control Specialist
Bereavement Counselor
Roadkill Remover
Asbestos Abatement Technician
Wet Nurse
Elder Abuse Investigator
Beekeeper
Fleshing Machine Operator
Pundit
Traffic Accident Investigator
Gynecological Oncologist
Webmaster
Maggot Farmer
Ethicist

Unfrozen

Delphi's thumb hovered over the holo-screen. In the clerk's shabby office, an old-fashioned poster of three kittens in a mailbox watched her from behind the clerk's bald head. Through the glass desk, Delphi watched him tapping his heel against the tile.

"Once you agree, the Unfrozen is your complete financial and legal responsibility," said the clerk in a practiced tone, "No matter their physical or mental condition, you must provide a safe and nurturing environment. Failure to follow these rules may result in surrender of the Unfrozen and fines of up to $800,000. Future Freeze Inc. is not liable for any damage the Unfrozen causes to you or your property."

On the holo-screen was a picture of a blonde woman sitting on a porch swing. Her white blouse was emblazoned with large golden sunflowers and her eyes gazed adoringly at someone out of frame. Next to the picture was her scant biographical information. Caroline Swisher, Age 34, Died July 19, 2025, Frozen July 20, 2025, Cause of Death Ovarian Cancer.

"I know what I'm getting into," said Delphi as she pressed the ID chip implanted in her thumb onto the holo-screen. Her Feed was jammed with countless stories of people unfreezing ancient relatives to have them become cherished members of their families. She'd wept through the documentary about the Unfrozen husband and wife, reunited a hundred and fifty years into the future. And everyone had read the memoir of the woman who learned to rediscover the wonder of the world by seeing it through her Unfrozen great to the seventh grandmother's eyes.

Even her cynical friend Vin, who had called getting an Unfrozen a "status symbol you had to teach to use the bathroom" had changed his mind when his sister Unfroze their great to the tenth grandfather. Now Vin's Feed was nothing but happy images of him with his Unfrozen. Pictures of them vacationing on the Moon, singing in the electro-chorus, and wearing matching shirts that made them look more like brothers than centuries distant relatives.

The holo-screen turned green, accepting Delphi's ID chip. She stared into Caroline's big blue eyes, so excited to meet this distant flesh and blood. Would she share Delphi's sense of humor? Her love of macadamia nuts? The ability to dance to anything, even hold music? She felt like an expectant parent, altering her home to give Caroline a space to sleep, wondering about her personality, and preparing herself for this new life that was her responsibility. Delphi was so excited, she had even purchased a sunflower to welcome Caroline into her new world, an expensive luxury after the latest Queensland drought.

"We'll start the thawing now. Should take about an hour," said the clerk. He scratched his moustache and waved her out of his office.

Delphi picked up her backpack and walked down a hallway to the waiting room. Through a large window she spied hundreds of eight foot tall metal cylinders. Which one contained her Caroline? She paused, imagining what was happening right now. Caroline was being woken up after two hundred years of cryogenic sleep and being told all about Delphi. She imagined their first embrace. Wrapping her arms around this new piece of herself. Family brought together by the wonders of technology. Maybe their story would be good enough to get their own documentary. Delphi and Caroline, sisters through time.

"The waiting room is the second door on the left," said a woman in red scrubs.

"Oh, thanks," said Delphi, stopping her reverie and continuing down the hall. A dozen barely padded plastic chairs were shoved haphazardly around the perimeter of the dank room.

Delphi sat in a chair and closed her eyes. The half-finished episode of *The Office* restarted in her mind. Ever since she'd petitioned for custody of Caroline, Delphi had been familiarizing herself with the culture Caroline had lived in. *The Office* was an old American documentary about life in a paper company. Delphi had only seen paper in museums, but in Caroline's time it was ubiquitous enough there were businesses whose sole mission was selling people reams of dead trees.

After the episode ended, Delphi opened the genetic results, marveling at the overlapping segments proving Caroline was family. Not close family, a fourth degree cousin. But, in the thirty days legally mandated after Delphi had made her claim, no one with a closer genetic match had petitioned for Caroline, making her Delphi's.

Delphi skimmed through the book she'd downloaded the night before, *The Care and Keeping of an Unfrozen.* The only living being Delphi had ever been in charge of was the small domestic wallaby her ex-partner had left behind in their tumultuous breakup. And even that stewardship only lasted two months until her ex came back for the wallaby and bag of drugs they'd kept under the mattress.

Delphi knew she would have to be patient with Caroline. She was from an age where people burned oil for fuel and every country had its own currency they carried on plastic cards. On *The Office* no one ate Corth (a nutrient-rich algae that was the base of most foods), put on a go-out (a rubber suit that protected one's skin from pollution), or had even heard of the Chinese American War (still happening seventy years later as a treaty had never officially been signed.) But a history lesson could come later. The moment she got Caroline home, she would give her a bath, put her in the plaid nightgown that matched Delphi's, hand her a mug of hot chocolate, and upload the charming tableau to her Feed. The likes and comments would flood in.

Beautiful! #UnfrozenGoals
Aww, you are so lucky.

Congratulations! My Unfrozen loves cocoa too. We should do a play date, haha!

"Knock knock," said the clerk as he peeked around the door, "Someone's excited to see you."

Delphi stood and put on her best Welcome to the Future smile. The clerk pulled the lead of a blue harness, strapped around the waist of a frail woman in a pale pink muumuu. The woman struggled and moaned as if every step broke another bone in her body. Her blonde hair, tangled into one huge mat, hung over her face, covering all but one roving blue eye.

"She's cancer-free and immunized. Bring her back in two months for her second round of shots and a dental cleaning. You can also bring her in for grooming, which we offer at a reasonable rate." The clerk yanked the leash, pulling Caroline in front of Delphi. "Caroline, this is your cousin Delphi. Remember, I told you you're going home with her."

Caroline winced as if the clerk had screamed, but nodded. The clerk handed the end of the blue lead to Delphi.

"Hi Caroline, we're going to have so much fun." Delphi didn't let Caroline's haggard appearance dampen her enthusiasm. A hot bath, some leave-in conditioner, and a hearty meal would put her right. "I made you a comfy bed on my couch and there are yummy snacks and cozy pajamas. And once you rest up, we'll go on walks and play games and be a real family." Delphi stroked Caroline's bony hand. "I can even take you to the Sydney Opera House. They had that in your time, right?"

Caroline reached out and touched Delphi's face. Her fingers were ice. "I'm in Sydney?" she said in a thin croak.

"Yes Caroline," said the clerk, "I told you already. You're going to need to listen better than that if you want to thrive here. Delphi, ping me if there are any problems. Oh, and here," the clerk handed her a white paper bag, "Some sedatives. You can hide one in a Corth bar if she's getting hard to handle."

The clerk gave her a tiny salute, turned on his heel, and left Delphi alone with her new relative. Delphi removed the blue lead from Caroline's waist. She felt ribs sticking out of

Caroline's disastrously thin frame. No matter, she'd have her fat and happy in no time. Freed from her harness, Caroline shuffled around the waiting room, her slippers slapping against the tile.

"Are you hungry, Caroline?" Delphi turned to retrieve a Corth bar from her backpack.

That's when Caroline lunged.

Her bony arms wrapped around Delphi's neck, twisting this way and that, like she was trying to pop the lid off a stubborn jar. Delphi stepped backward, trying to shake off the skeletal parasite, but Caroline clamped on harder, sinking her teeth into the back of Delphi's neck.

"Who the fuck are you?" Caroline croaked, "Where's Sean? Tell me where my fucking family is." Caroline loosened her grip on Delphi's neck to allow her to speak.

"I'm Delphi. I'm your family." Blood trickled down her neck. This was not how it was supposed to go. This was supposed to be a warm fuzzy scene of reuniting of distant relatives, not a scene of unprovoked violence. Maybe something had gone wrong with Caroline's unfreezing. The sweet, good natured part of her brain still coated in freezer burn. A dose of reality would shake Caroline from her haze. "They're dead. All the people you know have been dead for two hundred years. You're mine now."

Caroline screeched, her long nails digging for Delphi's eyes. Delphi clawed at Caroline's matted head, clumps of hair getting tangled between her fingers. Spots of darkness danced in her vision as her brain was deprived of oxygen. She tried to shake Caroline off her back, but she only clung on tighter.

"I didn't ask for this," Caroline hissed into Delphi's ear, "I don't want-"

All at once, Caroline's body detached. A soft thunk on the tile. Delphi gasped, choking down air to replenish her oxygen starved cells. The clerk stood in the doorway holding a black remote in his hand.

"Sorry about that," said the clerk, "Nothing in her record suggested a violent personality. She was so docile for me, I thought she'd be alright." He handed Delphi an Insta Heal patch for her bleeding neck.

Caroline's body lay between them, her dry limbs curled like a dead spider's. In death, her face no longer twisted into a suspicious snarl, she resembled the smiling woman in the photo.

"Does that happen a lot?" asked Delphi. She'd never heard of an Unfrozen getting violent. Vin's posts about his great-grandpa had been so serene. Why would anyone be angry at being given a new chance at life?

"We have an extermination rate of six percent. It's why we started implanting every Unfrozen with a kill chip. It was such a mess doing it by hand." The clerk waved in the woman in the red scrubs.

Delphi remembered the sunflower in her backpack. She held it out to the woman. "This was for her."

"I wouldn't waste a flower on the incinerator."

"Then you keep it. I don't want it." The optimism of that morning, spending half her week's paycheck on a gift, was replaced by bitter disappointment.

The woman took the flower. In a practiced scoop, she threw Caroline's body over her shoulder and disappeared through the door.

"Don't blame yourself," said the clerk, "Some don't un-freeze correctly. Most of the time it's obvious and we extermin-ate immediately. You're lucky Caroline sprung on you when she did."

"Lucky?" Tears stung Delphi's eyes. She'd told everyone she was getting an Unfrozen and now she was going home empty handed. How would she explain that her beloved Caro-line had turned out to be a murderous monster? Delphi dreaded going home to her Caroline-proofed apartment alone. Lonely for a person she'd never really had.

"Yes lucky," said the clerk, "Lucky she didn't wait until you got her home."

Delphi imagined those bony fingers snaking around her neck while she slept. Lucky was the right word.

"I can offer you a refund of your adoption fee, minus the cost of the kill chip, or I can give you credit for another Un-frozen."

"Another?"

"According to your file, you're a genetic match to Sydney Hunter." The clerk held up a holo-screen with a picture of a woman with wavy brown hair holding a big scoop of ice cream. "She's frozen in The American Federation, but after all you've gone through, we'd be happy to waive the shipping fee."

Delphi's first instinct was to refuse. Why allow herself to be disappointed again? Then she looked at Sydney. Her goofy grin making dimples on her plump cheeks. Dimples just like the ones Delphi got when she genuinely smiled. A rush of certainty. Sydney was family. Delphi could see it now. The two of them wrapped in matching paisley robes, standing on a balcony at sunset, arms wrapped around each other, smiling so hard their dimples hurt.

Disney Cruise Announcements From The Bermuda Triangle

Hey there, Party Princes and Princesses! I'm Jimmy, aka your Cruise Director. We just left port in New York City and are on our way to the gorgeous island of Bermuda. Enjoy your time on The Disney Magic, where all your cruise dreams come true.

What's up, my 101 Cruise-Mations! A tropical storm is in our path, so captain's orders, we're headed south to avoid it. That gives everyone more time to enjoy the soft serve at Mike Wazowski's Eye Scream Treats.

Good evening, my Bedknobs and Broomsticks! Our on-board technology is acting a little Goofy, so we will not be screening *Beauty and the Beast* in The Buena Vista Theater. Also, if any guests have brought their own GPS systems aboard, we ask that you give them to a Disney team member. You'll receive a Rose Gold Minnie Mouse Headband if your GPS shows anything other than a never-ending expanse of gray static.

Hey, it's Jimmy. We're overwhelmed by the reports of missing children. Especially because we've gotten more reports than children listed on the ship's manifest. We kindly ask every passenger to remember how many children they brought with them onto the ship. For a rough estimate, count the number of children's shoes in your room and divide by two.

Good afternoon, my Beasts and Beauties! We'll be having our Princess's Royal Tea in fifteen minutes at the Royal Court Restaurant. We welcome any prince or princess to join us for a magical teatime experience.

So sorry we had to cut the Royal Tea short. And apologies to any passengers startled by the screams. For those who weren't there, every participant in the Royal Tea saw a shared vision of an ancient city plunging into the sea as they felt as though they were simultaneously burning to death and drowning alive. We also apologize that we ran out of tiaras.

Hey there, my Winnie-the-Cruises! You should not trust compasses given out as part of the Pirates of the Caribbean experience. Several passengers have followed the compasses to the bowels of the ship and have not been seen since.

An update: Those who followed their compasses have returned and are standing in a circle in the Vibe Youth Club chanting Vibe, Vibe, Vibe, in frantic tones.

Hey my Delightful Dinglehoppers! A word of warning that the Aqua Dunk water slide has sealed itself shut. Unfortunately, staff discovered this after eight children had become jammed together at the bottom. We have made multiple rescue attempts, but the end of the slide is impervious to our tools. We tried lowering down a rope, but it came back frayed as though it had been chewed by enormous jaws. So watch out for that!

FYI! Passengers should avoid the rats streaming out of every toilet on the ship. They are not Remy from Disney Pixar's Ratatouille. Though, yes, they do all have the face of Patton Oswalt.

An update on those missing children reports. Turns out, most of them were made by tortured souls searching for children long dead and lost to the sea. So, that's a mystery solved!

Hey there! A few wise guys have been saying the Bermuda Triangle is caused by nothing more than methane gas pockets and inclement weather. Those smart alecks have been strung up in Pinocchio's Pizzeria as an offering to whatever God will help us to safety.

We have cancelled this afternoon's costumed character

meet and greet. All characters have gone (hopefully temporarily) insane. On a personal note, I had been seeing Rapunzel, and it wasn't anything serious, but having a woman who's watched you cry after passionate whoopie, try to strangle you with her ten-foot-long wig has left this cruise director shaken up.

Just letting everyone know that last night, the captain spotted another ship. We attempted a distress call and set off the last of our Mickey fireworks to get their attention. The other ship ignored our calls and instead sailed straight through us. Not sure if *it* was a ghost ship or *we* are a ghost ship. But frankly, neither option is a comfort.

I've been thinking about death. It's something we humans take for granted. That no matter how much suffering we experience in this life it will come to an end. It's strange to be grateful for death, but here we are. Wondering if we will reach that most human of ending points. Or will we be here, suspended forever, dancing the Mickey Slide into eternity?

Hey there, my Guardians of the Galax-Sea! Those passengers gathered in the Vibe Lounge were onto something, and their rhythmic chants have guided us back to New York City. For those passengers dissatisfied with their journey, we will offer 10% off ALL items at our on-ship boutiques. And thanks for taking a cruise on The Disney Magic!

Cooper's Hawk

I'm pushing my tapioca pudding around my plate with my safety spork when I hear her. Pearl. A laugh like a cartoon kitten on helium. Even though I haven't heard that laugh in fifty years, it pulls me back to the fish stick scented hallways of Topeka High School. I'd turn to look, but I can't turn my neck that far without arthritis pain shooting up my spine. And more importantly, I don't want to give that bitch the satisfaction.

"She's new," comments Berta, my dull mealtime companion clad in a stained Looney Tunes t-shirt. The churn of lives in and out of the nursing home is nothing new. I'm furious at Berta for noticing *her* arrival. No one should comment on the tide after days on the ocean.

"We hate her," I say, forcing Berta's wet gaze to meet mine across the cafeteria table, "We hate her."

"Oh, okay," says Berta. It's hard to tell what gets through, but with repetition, you can usually make a message stick. It had taken weeks, but now Berta no longer prefers the seat next to the big window and I get to spend my afternoons watching the birds flit back and forth at the bird feeder. Berta didn't even appreciate the birds; not like I do.

A few weeks after I arrived here, I discovered the bird window. It's a large picture window in the East Lounge that looks out on the field behind the nursing home where two large bird feeders are stuck into the ground next to a small pond. I'd been in a slump, depressed over landing myself in the Grim Reaper's waiting room, but the birds give me something to do. I called my son and asked him to send me a guide to the birds of Kansas and a pair of binoculars, and I'm checking off birds as I see them.

Thankfully, they wheel *her* to a different dinner table, and I am not forced to confront my demon over tonight's runny meatloaf. I need time to prepare. I need to build up my strength. Instead of moving my food across my plate to make it look as though I've eaten it, I shovel in bite after bite. Even though it tastes like soggy sewage and every chew and swallow makes my jaw ache and my throat burn, I eat it all.

"Wowzah Mabel! Someone's appetite is improving," says tattooed Erika, the third most annoying aide. She sticks a green sticker to my wool sweater that says, "Clean Plate Club" and features an empty dinner plate giving a thumb's up.

I smile and pretend to admire the sticker as if it isn't infantilizing to praise a seventy-three-year-old woman for eating dinner. Erika grins back and gives me a thumbs up, the same as the dinner plate. If she knew the reason I cleaned my plate, I doubt she'd be grinning. Because I'm going to need all the energy I can get to kill Pearl Sherwood.

Watching and listening for Pearl has invigorated the typical drudgery of my daily routine. At breakfast, I eat my lump of oatmeal with verve. I take my cupful of pills (hiding the Risperdal and Aricept under my tongue and spitting it into my napkin.) My mind is as sharp as a buzz saw, but you wouldn't know it from my medical chart.

On Monday and Thursday mornings I have art class. Though, both the words art and class are applied too generously to the cramped room of coffin dodgers dumbly swirling oil pastels on construction paper. This week we are working on still life drawings of fruit. The art teacher is a bony community college dropout who spends most of the class on her phone arguing with her child's father about how late he stays out with his boys. She piles leftover fruit from the cafeteria on our tables each day, paying no attention to keeping the amount or arrangement consistent. One day is a banana, an apple, and a pear. Next, the pear is now three oranges, and the banana is half-rotten.

Normally this sloppiness would irk me, but today I am untouchable. As I try to incorporate the new green apple into my drawing, my mind cycles through possibilities of where

Pearl could be. Perhaps she chose music, or she has afternoon art. Or she's injured and needs intense physical therapy. Or maybe she has refused classes, saying we're all beneath her and demanding private lessons. It's a very Pearl thing to do.

Afternoons I spend watching the birds. It's April, as every oversized calendar and springtime decoration meant to give residents a sense of the passage of time informs me. Today, I see all manner of warblers, sparrows, chickadees, jays, and even a cardinal. My favorite bird is a Cooper's hawk that sometimes sits on top of the electric pole across the road. Once I sat watching him for three hours until he swooped down and grabbed a mouse from the grass. I have always admired the patience of skilled hunters.

My schedule does not overlap with Pearl's. I glimpse her at mealtimes, but we're always at opposite sides of the crowded cafeteria. My other opportunity for intelligence gathering is the aides. Normally, I tune out the banal gossip of the also-rans getting paid $7.25 an hour to make sure I'm minimally comfortable in purgatory. All week, I keep my ears open, but beyond the necessary - Mr. Thompson needs his insulin, Someone's been eating puzzle pieces again, We're out of catheters in D-wing - they don't talk about us. Pearl's arrival is only important in that she has filled the spot left by another sad sack of guts who's now providing dinner to some lucky worms. So I have to wait, hoping the hand of fate that has brought us back together after all these years keeps pushing.

Saturday afternoon is my monthly visit to the beauty parlor. Unlike most of the blue hairs in here, I have kept my hair long. I allow a trim, but never above my shoulders. I spend most of my time in the beauty parlor reading the months old gossip magazines from the bin in the corner. Trashy, I know, but fascinating to see what passes for clothing these days. As I'm reading about how the stars are like me, I see her. Crucifix-wearing Marquis, the eighth most annoying aide, wheels her into the dingy beauty parlor to wait her turn.

"Is this the hair salon?" Pearl asks Marquis, judgment dripping from her tongue. This is the first time I've gotten a good look at her. Her skin is less wrinkled than mine, but only because she's gotten fat. The nose that was slightly too big for her face in her youth, now overwhelms her. And her teeth are most definitely dentures.

"Yep, you'll come here once a month to get your hair done. Isn't that a treat?" Marquis looks for a space to park Pearl and wheels her right next to me. "Pearl, this is Mabel. She's an old pro at the salon. If you have questions, ask her."

Pearl turns her chunky head to me, ears flapping like Dumbo, and smiles. "I'm Pearl. What's your name?"

That bitch. That unrepentant, vile snake in the grass. She knows exactly who I am. This innocent act might fool everyone else in this place, but I see right through her from her overpermed head to her Velcro Clark's clad feet. She hasn't changed a bit since high school. Still dressing for attention in a tight pink sweatshirt featuring three kittens in a mailbox, the sexual message clear as day.

Her hand trembles as she points at a picture on my magazine. "That's my grandson."

I flip to the cover. Could this putrid wench have spawned a celebrity? She's pointing to a red haired man above the caption "Harry's Secret Struggles." I flip to the inside and find this "Harry" is Prince Harry. I almost laugh. Pearl is trying to convince me she's the Queen of England? She thinks I'm dumb enough to fall for that?

She giggles at me, her titter high enough to attract dogs. I imagine grabbing a pair of shears from the blue jar of Barbicide and jamming them into the side of her neck, piercing her carotid artery. I'd hold the shears there, letting her realize what had happened, feel the pain of the metal slicing her nerves, then rip out the scissors, letting the dam of blood spurt, splattering everyone in the salon. Those last satisfying gurgles, as her heart kept pumping her blood, the muscle that had kept her alive so long, betraying her at the end.

But even if I wanted to, I can't do it. I'm too weak. I curse the incident that sent me here. On the outside I was strong, taking daily walks and lifting my hand weights while I watched Jeopardy. I'd always been big, on the north side of six foot and built like a Viking bride. Inside the nursing home, I have atrophied. My legs wobble after a few steps and my hands struggle to grasp. It's all her fault.

I nod at Pearl and say, "Oh, that's nice."

I spend the rest of my afternoon fantasizing about pushing Pearl off the top floor of buildings in exotic locales.

Three geezers have died from the flu this week, so they put us on lockdown. The last gasp of a particularly deadly flu season. This means staying in my room 24/7. No classes, meals delivered to me, no contact with anyone but the staff. I'm lucky to have a private room. Helping two sons through law school has paid off.

Most of my day I listen to audiobooks on my daughter's old iPad. I'm omnivorous in my listening habits. From Agatha Christie to Colson Whitehead to Stephen King, I'll listen to anything my unlimited Audible subscription allows. While I listen, I look out the window. Unfortunately, my room is on the other side of the building from the bird feeder. All I can see over here is an empty cornfield, not yet ready for planting. My mind wanders. I think about Pearl, cataloging every scrap of information I have floating in my mind, sifting for anything useful. It's hard to be inspired in between these four peach colored walls. I always did my best thinking on my feet.

Did I always hate her? No, before eleventh grade I barely noticed her. She was another empty headed hussy flitting around the school with her pack of equally dimwitted girlfriends. But then she caught my attention. It was during English class. Mrs. Elmer asked me to come to the front of the class and recite a piece of The Iliad. I always had an excellent memory. As I returned to my desk I didn't notice Pearl sneaking behind me, pulling out my chair as I sat down. I hit the floor with a thunk, knocking the breath from my lungs. I shrieked in fear, scrabbling around on the dirty linoleum, the animal part of my brain ready for further attack.

The entire class erupted in laughter as Pearl stood above me, laughing so hard that spittle ran down her chin, hitting me on the forehead. This braying ass had made me look foolish. Even Mrs. Elmer, my second favorite teacher, giggled as she scolded Pearl for her prank. All I wanted to do was kick Pearl's spindly legs out from under her and make her feel the humiliation I felt. But I pretended to laugh along.

From that moment forward, every memory I have of her is tinged with red. Pearl giggling when I dropped my frog in biology class. Calling me Elephant Legs because I towered over the girls, the boys, and most of the teachers in school. The way Mr. Brenner chose her for President of English club so he could spend every day after school with Pearl's perky tits, even though I had the highest grade in class. Pearl is not the only person I hated in high school. I hated everyone, except for Arthur Goodwin, whose limbs had shriveled from Polio and who was altogether too pathetic to hate. But she is the only one who ever made me feel weak.

When gap-toothed Leelee, the most annoying aide, brings me my dinner, she pauses to talk. This is what makes her the most annoying, the constant chatter. Her mouth is a faucet, every thought pouring out. Tonight, I will divert the flow in my direction.

"Leelee," I say as she puts the tray of slop on my table, "I was hoping you could help me with something."

"Oh Mabel, did you make a mess?"

"Not that." Humiliating that she assumes I've soiled myself, but I continue. "I was wondering about a new girl, Pearl Sherwood, over in B-Hall. See, we were best friends in high school."

And that's all she needs. The floodgates open. Twaddle about how adorable it is and maybe they can put our story in the spring newsletter, but I extract a few useful tidbits. Pearl was living in Milwaukee, but she had a stroke and her younger sister brought her to live closer to home. Her husband, Lou Bozarth, had died of cancer three years earlier.

So, she married Lou. A rude beanstalk of a boy whose best quality was his family's wealth. But she had gotten out, at least as far as Milwaukee. While I rotted on the vine in Topeka until I said yes to the first dolt to ask the question and popped out three crumb snatchers. But I made my own life, didn't I? No one would think it looking in from the outside, but I had my fun.

Our first meal back in the cafeteria is tense. Two weeks in isolation has made everyone cranky. Mummies disturbed from our tombs. I'm scanning the cafeteria for Pearl, so caught up in my search I don't notice Berta is swiping my graham crackers. I'm about to snarl at her, when I see Pearl being wheeled in by Leelee. The flu hasn't claimed her life before I can. Leelee spots me and wheels Pearl over to my table.

"Since, you girls are friends, I put you on the same activity schedule and you'll be meal buddies. How does that sound?"

"Wonderful, thank you," I say, "It's such a pleasure to be reunited with an old friend."

"Old friends are like gold," says Pearl, "You need them to hold your diamonds."

Being anchored to Pearl is both a blessing and a curse. Blessing, because I have a million opportunities to watch her, study her, work out my plan to kill her. Curse, because I must spend so much time with her. She's needy, constantly asking questions, pretending she doesn't understand things to get more attention from the aides, complaining about this pain or that ache. For eleven days, her words grate my brain, leaving my mind in furious shreds I must piece together at night to be ready for the next day's assault. Until I discover my game.

We're at the bird window. Even my formerly solitary pleasures are haunted by her loathsome presence. I'm looking up a bird I don't recognize, a stripy woodpecker, hoping it's a Williamson's Sapsucker and I can cross it off my bird list. Right when I get to the correct page and try to compare the bird to the book's illustration, Pearl asks, "Where's Lou?"

"What?" I turn on reflex and the bird flies away. Damn it.

"Where's Lou? He's my husband." Pearl swivels her head pathetically, as if he's about to appear from behind the wilted potted palm.

"Quiet Pearl," I say, "We're here to look at the birds."

"Is Lou coming? He's supposed to take me to the movies tonight." She grasps at my arm with her greasy sausage fingers.

I jerk my arm away and spit, "Lou's dead. He's never coming to take you to the movies because he's dead. D. E. A. D. Dead."

Grief and shock play over her hideous face. Her bottom lip trembles and tears leak from her rheumy eyes. She hangs her head and weeps into her lap. None of the aides come to check on her. Emotional outbursts are only a problem if they're disruptive.

I return to my bird watching until thirty minutes later, she asks again, "Where's Lou? Is he coming soon?"

"No Pearl," I sigh, putting down my binoculars, "Lou's never coming for you. He's dead."

"Lou's- he's...." Fresh tears follow the tracks of the ones spilled before them.

"Uh huh, he was eaten by a bear. A big old grizzly ripped him apart and played Parcheesi with his gallbladder." She falls silent again, grieving beside me. I get another half hour of peace.

Over the next few days Lou dies from cancer, gunshot, fire, drowning, suicide, cirrhosis, falling off a roof, poison, heart disease, eaten by cannibals, falling into a vat of chocolate, and accidental strangulation from autoerotic asphyxiation. I'm a kid with a jack-in-the-box. I know what's going to happen every time, but I never tire of playing. It's fun, but I'm keeping my primary goal in focus. However, if I can make her last days on Earth as distressing as possible, that's the scoop of ice cream on top of my pernicious pie.

On Friday I receive a call from my son, Arthur. It's short,

both of us trying to end the call as quickly as possible without offending the other. I have three children. They call once a week, taking turns between them. They talk about their lives and I ask for what I need, more books, a heavier blanket, a chain for my glasses that doesn't get caught in my hair. Regrettably, they all take after their father. The two boys, Douglas and Arthur, have a dash of me, the cunning to be bigshot corporate lawyers, but the girl, Karen, is all sugar and frills, an elementary school librarian in Oregon married to a philosophy professor. I'd be disappointed if I cared.

I gave them a Norman Rockwell childhood. My husband worked his way up the ladder at the Frito-Lay plant while I stayed home reproducing salads I saw in magazines. Every lunch was packed with care, every scraped knee kissed, every Christmas letter bragged of the littlest one playing piano or the big one being elected student council president. Early on, I decided that if I was going to indulge the inside part of me, the outside had to be pristine.

Never a hair out of place. A loyal wife that no one would raise an eyebrow at offering a ride to a drifter looking to get into town because she's just so kind. A woman no one would pay any mind to buying new kitchen knives every few months because of all those meals she cooks for the poor folks at the church. Not a blink of suspicion at this mother offering a down on his luck Vietnam Vet position at her brother's building company in Kansas City. A pillar of the community so burnished on her exterior no one noticed the inside was all wet leaves and asbestos.

"Knock, knock," says Dr. Kim as he enters my room for my monthly check-up. He's handsomely dressed, in a pristine white coat over his green polo and khaki Dockers.

"Good afternoon, Doctor," I say.

Dr. Kim is a smart man. A doctor, an art lover, a polyglot. The first time he visited, he noticed my Kandinsky wall calendar. Not the typical Thomas Kinkade junk hanging in every other mouth-breathing pudding zombie's room. I can tell he enjoys his visits with me, because we can have an intelligent conversation.

"My wife and I were in Kansas City and went to the funniest museum," he says as he takes my vitals, "I thought you'd appreciate hearing about it."

"Where did you and Lisa go?" I ask. His wife Lisa is a pretty Korean American OBGYN. He lights up whenever he talks about her. I try not to picture her getting dropped in a giant meat grinder too often.

"It was a hair museum. Hundreds of intricate floral wreaths and jewelry all made of human hair. It was a Victorian mourning ritual." He puts the blood pressure cuff around my arm and inflates it.

"It makes sense. To want to keep a piece of a person who meant something to you." I think about the lockbox under my bed. Full of keys. House keys, car keys, mailbox keys. Even when a person has left the locks behind, they hold on to the key, always hoping they'll be back to open them.

"I told Lisa she'd better get a lock of mine now, if she wants enough to make a bracelet." He rubs the growing bald spot on the top of his head. "But Mabel, you could make a whole wreath with all your hair."

I grin and run a finger through my long silver locks. If only I were forty years younger.

"Blood pressure is a bit high, so I'm upping your dose of Vasotec. You're still sharp as a tack, so the anti-dementia drugs must be doing their job. Anything you want to ask me?"

I can't think of any way to make him stay longer without getting myself put on another medication, so I say, "No. Thank you very much." And I actually mean it.

Every day I feel the pressure. The god awful tick tock of the hands of time. Any day Pearl could have a heart attack or take a fall or catch a cold. Nature could steal away my chance to commit my final sin.

At breakfast, I consider poison. The coward's device. Such

a simple thing to steal pills from an unwatched tray, grind them up, and sprinkle them on her eggs. I'd always heard poison was the choice of women. Its neatness. The lack of contact. How easy for the head of the domestic sphere to corrupt her own domain. The closest I'd ever gotten to poisoning anyone was slipping half a sleeping pill in my kid's milk before naptime. I would not let myself go out with a whimper. No poison.

During art, I think about stabbing. My area of expertise, if I do say so myself. Swiping a knife from the kitchen would be hard, but not impossible. This isn't prison. No one is worried about us shriveled prunes stabbing each other during Therapy Dog Thursday. The only thing stopping me from doing it is the reality of getting caught. A stabbed drifter buried in the woods was one thing, but a stabbed old lady in a nursing home will be investigated. And as soul-sucking as my life has become, I still value the freedom I have.

As I watch the birds, I think about asphyxiation. If I flip her over, make it seem as though she got tangled in her blankets and wasn't able to turn herself, her death would be seen as an unfortunate accident. Us decrepit crones are constantly keeling over without investigation. My only worry is my strength. A few months ago I would have been confident in my arms' ability to press her body into the bed, but now my hands tremble when I brush my hair for too long. The humiliating thought of Pearl overpowering me is too much to bear.

On Friday, they stuff us into the largest common room to watch young people sing a cappella versions of 50s and 60s hits. By the mercy of a nonexistent God, I am not sat next to Pearl. Instead, I am wheeled between two boiled vegetables who don't make a peep during the whole embarrassing spectacle.

The kids are from the local high school. Probably volunteering to do something that'll look good on college applications. Clean cut and pimply, they gesticulate through Elvis and The Supremes. A short, freckled girl in a blue dress introduces each number, saying something asinine.

"I bet you remember putting on your Bobby socks and

dancing to this number."

"I bet this takes you back to the Summer of Love."

"I bet this next one was a favorite on the jukebox at your local malt shop."

I'm not the only one who finds the girl grating. Every time she speaks, a black girl with a nose ring rolls her eyes from the chorus. Typically, I find facial jewelry tacky, but the pure loathing the girl has for little miss freckles makes me like her. When the freckled girl's voice cracks, trying to hit a high note, both of us snicker at her failure.

After the concert is over, they force the kids to mingle with us. Nose ring positions herself in the back corner, near me and the vegetables, surreptitiously looking at her phone. Freckles is taking selfies with the old codgers as they paw at her, trying to grasp at their stolen youth. Pearl wheels right up to Freckles. It is like seeing the past and the present, young girl and old woman at opposite ends of their lives, both unrepentant cunts.

I wheel over to Nose Ring. She smells of vanilla body spray and hormonal sweat. She sees me approach, but her eyes stay on her phone.

"You have a lovely singing voice," I say. At her age I would have eaten up the compliment, but she just shrugs. "What's your name?"

"I'm Mallory." Her manners kick in. "What's your name?"

"Mabel." She looks up from her phone. Pure disgust. I'm the specter of a future she doesn't want to think about. "How old are you, Mallory?"

"Uh, sixteen. How old are you?" What a bitch. I love her.

"Seventy-three." I'm about to ask her about Freckles, but the chaperone calls for the kids to get on the bus.

"Halle-fucking-lujah," says Mallory. She snakes her way through the sea of almost-corpses. Despite myself, my arm reaches out, trying to hold on to her. Don't go. Don't leave. We could be friends, you and me. I could teach you so much. How to harness your disgust with the world and use it. That the secret to getting through the interminable slog of living with the cretinous blobs surrounding you is to eliminate the ones that irk you most. The drunks, the suck-ups, the numbskulls. The detritus sucking up oxygen they don't deserve. She glances back and sees my pathetic gesture, and her whole body spasms with repugnance.

And I'm there again. Reaching out to the girl from the side of the road. Offering money, candy, whatever she wanted. Begging, pleading that she not tell anyone. She looks at me, the weak sniveling creature laying in a ditch, with the same look as Nose Ring. Like she's stepped on a dead squirrel on the sidewalk, its entrails gushing out from both ends. It's the look I'd give a man before plunging a knife through his breastbone. To be seen as pathetic, weak, dumb. I hate it. I want to rise out of my chair, wrap my hands around Nose Ring's throat, and watch her disgust turn to fear. To feel her pulse crescendo under my palms then slow and slow and stop. To show every person in this room that I am powerful. I am strong. I am terrible.

But I can't.

I'm a zombie through dinner. The memory rises. A flood, paralyzing my legs, stopping my heart, choking my throat. I shovel in my chicken fried steak, swallow all my pills, and ask to be taken to my room. I need to be alone. To allow the memory to overwhelm my senses, then recede like the tide.

I'm driving down 29th street. Passing the Methodist church headed toward the Post Office. I'm on my way to mail Christmas presents. Checks for the kids, stuffed animals for the grandkids, boxes of homemade fudge for everyone. I try to live up to that World's Best Grandma mug sitting in my cabinet. Eartha Kitt asks Santa for a '54 convertible on the radio. It's thirty degrees, and the sky is spitting snow. That's when I see her.

Impractically dressed in a tie dye t-shirt and cut-offs standing on the side of the road with her thumb stuck out. Hitchhiking? Kids don't hitchhike anymore. No one gets in a car with a stranger unless they've summoned them on their phone. Judging by her lack of winter clothes, she's desperate. A run- away. With no friend in the world to give her a ride.

I continue to the post office, mailing my packages but unable to stop thinking about the girl. She's not my usual type. I had planned for Dean to be the last one. A frail alcoholic who whispered lewd secrets to the church ladies at the soup kitchen. His death had been a blessing to everyone, especially himself. I'd locked up my box of keys, satisfied with a job well done. DNA, camera phones, GPS. Technology I was too old to learn how to outsmart.

But I'm bored. My husband is dead (heart attack, I swear). My kids have scattered like baby spiders on the wind. There's only so much Wheel of Fortune one can watch without wanting to drag someone through the forest by their hair and stab them until the dirt goes red. I circle the block three times, agonizing over my choice. I don't have a plan. I always have a plan. But the girl's defiant stupidity irks me.

"Do you need a ride, sweetie?" I roll down the passenger window, bitter wind blasting into my car's warm interior.

"Yuh huh," says the girl. Her lips are turning blue and her knobby knees clack together as she shivers.

"Get on in here." I unlock the passenger door and roll up the window. No hesitation to climb in the Buick driven by a kind old grandma. "Where are you headed?"

"Manhattan."

"My oh my, big city dreams."

She shakes her head, her seashell choker clacking. "Man- hattan, Kansas. That's where my dad lives with his girlfriend."

I get on 70 West. It's an hour to Manhattan from Topeka. While I drive, Bing Crosby dreams of a white Christmas and the girl chatters about her bitch mom and her bullshit rules and how at her dad's place there's always weed, and she can have boys over whenever she wants. What a piece of shit. Run- ning away from home at Christmas to get high and get laid. Her mother will be better off without the inevitable teen pregnancy and overdose in this girl's future.

We glide down the highway until I see a familiar exit that leads straight into the middle of nowhere. My turn signal is on and I'm turning right off the highway through forests and farms. I pull off the road in a quiet spot. Only when I park does the girl stop talking, realizing this is not Manhattan.

"Where are we?" she asks. Bobby Helms sings The Jingle Bell Rock until I turn off the car. She's scared. I can smell it. The animal fear leaking out of her pores. That teen overconfidence gone. She takes off her seatbelt and opens the passenger door.

"Thanks for the ride. I can- I can get out here."

My fingers grasp at her t-shirt but aren't strong enough to hold her. I undo my seatbelt and get out of the car.

Stupid, stupid, stupid. Coming out here with no plan. No weapon. No alibi. The girl springs across the ditch along the road and into a barren corn field, her feet crunching on the frosty earth. I run after her. My slip-on clogs offer no traction. As I approach the incline of the ditch, my foot slips on a patch of ice and I slam to the ground and roll to the bottom into a tangle of muddy weeds.

Dumb fucking twat. Stupid bitch. Dimwit cretin. I curse at the girl and myself. My breath bubbles. I'm drowning. I'll discover later a broken rib has punctured my lung. Above me, the girl's face eclipses the sun.

"Are you okay?" she asks, leaning over to help me out of the ditch.

I grab at her pigtails, trying to drag her down with me.

"Fuck, what's wrong with you?" She steps out of my reach.

We're both shivering with cold and fear. She takes a flip phone from her pocket and calls 911. I beg her to stop. Help me back into the car and I'll take her anywhere she wants to go. The ambulance siren grows louder. I pray for the ground to open and swallow me whole. Bury me in the frozen dirt. It's all ahead of me. The interrogation room, the tiny cell, telling so many parents where their wayward sons are buried so I can avoid the sting of the needle as they put me down like a rabid dog.

But it doesn't happen. I don't go to jail, but the hospital, where my sentence is not life without the possibility of parole, but dementia. They call my kids. My sons are busy, but my daughter flies in long enough to pick out the nursing home that smells least like urine. I assume they send the girl home with a stern warning about not accepting rides from strangers. No one thinks I meant to hurt her. That I meant for her to stay in the corn field forever.

Is this why I haven't yet killed Pearl? Am I avoiding the feeling of impotence I felt laying in that icy ditch? The same thing I felt laying on the slick floor of Mrs. Elmer's classroom. The feeling that the tables had been so viciously turned. The lion taunted by the baby gazelle. I'd always been smarter, stronger, better than my prey. To be taken out by a mouthy teen wasn't the way it was supposed to end.

It reminds me of when my eldest son Douglas was eleven. He was scared to walk home from school alone because he had to pass our neighbor's rottweiler who barked at everyone who passed the yard. My first instinct was to feed the mutt a hamburger full of rat poison, but I decided instead to teach Douglas a lesson. One day after he had arrived home late again, having taken the longer route home to avoid the dog, I took him by the arm and dragged him to the neighbor's yard. The dog barked and growled, throwing itself against the fence, trying to reach Douglas. He cried and begged, but I held him against the fence, his face an inch from the dog's sharp teeth.

"Mommy, please," he said, "I'm scared."

"If you don't want to be scared, be scary. Go on. Bark back." I howled and barked at the dog, Douglas soon joining me.

His fists shook the fence as he screamed and growled at the startled dog which turned tail and ran into its doghouse. Douglas never avoided the house again. He learned to fight fear with fear.

I've forgotten this lesson. I'm afraid of failing to kill Pearl. The only thing that will defeat this fear is the fear in her eyes when I succeed.

By the time the sun sets, I can breathe again. I jam my nose into the bowl of lemon zest potpourri on my dresser. The acid sting clears the memory from my head. Tattooed Erika comes in and helps me into my pajamas.

"Did you hear the announcement at dinner, Mabel?" she asks.

"No," I say. I'm barely listening, more interested in trying to figure out the Latin phrase wrapped around the moon on Erika's arm, *Ad Astra per Aspera.*

"Next Saturday there's going to be a field trip to the Evel Knievel Museum. You know, the motorcycle guy? There's only twenty spots on the sign-up, so you'd better get a move on if you want to go." My idiotic Snoopy pajamas are on and Erika helps me into bed.

"I'll think about it." Astra means stars.

"I'm gonna go. A bunch of other aides are going too. This place is gonna be a ghost town without us." She hands me my iPad and earbuds to listen to an audiobook before I fall asleep. This kindness reshuffles my most hated aide rankings.

"I'll see if I feel up to it." The phrase is so familiar. To the stars roughly? I've seen it on a license plate, maybe.

Erika leaves, turning off the lights and shutting the door, before I have a chance to ask what her tattoo means. She probably doesn't even know. I once asked a man if he knew what the *Sic Semper Tyrannis* written across his chest meant. He didn't and was out of time to learn.

The choice between the field trip and the near-empty nursing home seems impossible. I run through pros and cons in my head all morning. The opportunity of a public space vs. the lack of supervision in an understaffed home. I'm so preoccupied, I can almost ignore Pearl blathering beside me. But of course. There's no need for me to decide. I'll go where Pearl goes.

On the Saturday of the field trip, all that's left are pudding brains, Pearl, and me. All the more senior aides have gone on the trip, leaving the less experienced ones to tend the vegetable

patch. I set my sights on Crystalynn, a buck-toothed girl fresh
from the farm who smells like manure and tells every female
resident she reminds her of her grandma.

Pearl and I are sitting at the bird window. I've refrained
from my game today, wanting Pearl happy and alert. I even include her in my bird spotting, allowing her to hold the field
guide.

"The birds are so pretty," she says. Then in a stunning moment of lucidity, "Reminds me of Mrs. Joiner's parrot who could
curse in every language. That bird called me a hussy in Russian
while I got my prom dress fitted."

I lower my binoculars to glare at her. This might seem like
an innocent memory, knocked loose by the flap of wings. But I
know better. As Pearl stood on Mrs. Joiner's pedestal, getting her
pink taffeta dress pinned, Mrs. Joiner was telling me she would
only make me a dress if I paid double. Pearl stifled her smile
as Mrs. Joiner said she'd have to use three times the fabric to
cover my "substantial frame." Having no other options, I'd had
to wear the plain black dress I'd bought for my father's funeral to
prom that year. Of course, Pearl is taunting me with this memory.

"Did you have fun at prom Pearl?" Keep it light. Crystalynn will come over to offer us afternoon snacks any minute.

"Oh yes, I love to dance. My husband and I went square
dancing every Friday night. Where is Lou? Is he here?"

I pray to the Gods of restraint. "He's on his way, Pearl.
You'll see him soon."

"Either of you want a snack? I have muffins and corn
chips." Crystalynn gestures to the snack tray she's put on the
table. The other aide on duty is busy helping feeble hands take
paper wrappers off blueberry muffins.

"Is it 2:30 already? We missed our outside time." I smile at
Crystalynn and look her straight in the eye, trying to look trust-
worthy and lucid.

"Outside time?" Crystalynn furrows her brow.

"Yes, ma'am. Pearl and I get outside to see the birds on Saturdays. Erika, the sweet girl with the tattoos, always takes us."

"Sorry, I'm so new. No one told me. Would it be ok if we go now?" The clunk of power shifts to my side of the scale.

"Of course, dear. I'll wheel myself and you push Pearl." Our little trio wheels toward the side door. Crystalynn punches in the door code (1492, which I of course knew already). I lead us along the concrete path past the bird feeder and toward the pond. I park myself as close to the pond as I can while remaining on the sidewalk, about six feet from the water's edge.

Crystalynn parks Pearl beside me. "How long does Erika usually let y'all stay out here?"

"It depends. Sometimes she combines outdoor time with a smoke break."

Crystalynn's fingers twitch. "Crap. If I'd known I would have brought my smokes." She looks around at the deserted pond. "They're in my car. You'll be ok if I leave you for a minute, right?"

"We'll be fine, won't we Pearl?"

Pearl, who is sniffing the air like a dog hanging out a car window, nods.

"Ok. Be back in a sec." Crystalynn jogs inside. She'll have to retrieve her keys from her locker, go out to her car for the cigarettes, go back in and put her keys away, then come back to us. I figure this will take about seven minutes. Fifteen, if she smokes a cigarette in her car.

I consider giving Pearl a speech about her cruelty coming back to haunt her. How she pulled my chair out from under me and how I'm about to do the same to her. I wish I could go back in time and tell that scared girl on the floor to be patient. It might take fifty years, but she would get her revenge. An ouroboros of cruelty and death. The moment where past meets present. Where beginning meets ending. Where actions beget consequences.

But I've never been one for dramatics. Signatures, letters to police, idiotic codes, only get you caught. I pull the brake on Pearl's wheelchair and she rolls forward. I put one arm on my wheel and one on the back of her chair and I slowly move us forward. My arms burn with effort, fighting to push all of Pearl's weight through the rough, muddy grass.

"Are we going fishing? Lou loves his walleye." She giggles as we reach the edge of the pond. The noise scrapes against my soul. "Hello, Mr. Fish."

Sweat is dripping into my eyes, my long hair stuck to my face. So close. The perfect last chapter to the story of my life. I wheel behind her and put my chair in park. Then I pull my arms back as far as I can and shove her chair forward. For a second, the chair hangs suspended, then her weight causes it to topple forward into the pond.

Pearl yells once before the wheelchair lands on top of her, weighing her down. It is a pity it can't be my body holding her head under the water but being the engine of the machine of her demise will have to be enough. I don't blink, wanting to etch every moment of this victory into my mind. The memory of that stupid tie-dye wearing girl overwritten with my final glory.

The bubbles stop. The only evidence remaining of the life drowned in the pond are the wheelchair tracks in the grass. I am light as a feather, free as a bird, giddy as a goose, as I roll back to the sidewalk. When Crystalynn returns, I'll tell her another aide took Pearl to the hair salon. Her disappearance will fall on Crystalynn's shoulders, but she's young. She'll find another soul sucking job in no time.

While I wait, I enjoy the spring breeze. Birds chatter and swoop around the bird feeder. An injured wren shrieks in the grass, its left wing bent back. I scan the horizon until I see it. The Cooper's hawk is sitting on a telephone pole. Still. Silent. Waiting to make his move.

Yelp Reviews Of A Chuck E. Cheese Haunted By The Spirit Of Princess Diana

★ ★ ★ ★ ★
Matt R.

Had my son's eighth birthday party here last weekend. Pizza, games, prizes, what more could you want? Staff was really attentive. Kept asking us to mention if we saw or felt anything unusual. Only thing unusual was how much fun my son was having!

Manager Joe F.

Glad you and your son had a Cheesy Time!

★ ★ ★ ☆ ☆
Sara C.

Brought my daughter and her friends for the afternoon. The girls had fun, but I choked after I found a huge sapphire ring in my pretzel bites. Complained to my waitress, Camilla, but she was distracted. She kept screaming, "It's not me. You've got the wrong one," into the ball pit. Overall, I'd come back, but only because my daughter had a good time.

Manager Joe F.

So sorry about your negative experience, Sara. We pride ourselves on our quality food offerings, and I assure you the ring you found was not placed there by our chefs. I've had a talk with Camilla about her behavior with customers, and again, I don't want to make excuses, but it really isn't her fault.

Sara C.

Thanks for your response, but putting blame on other people isn't good management.

Manager Joe F.

Hey Sara. Don't mean to be rude here, but some situations ARE beyond our control. Really don't want to get metaphysical on Yelp, but rest assured we are taking steps to rectify the situation.

★ ★ ★ ★ ☆
Eric W.

Haven't been since I was a kid myself, but just like I remembered. My kids had a blast and my wife loved that this location served wine ;) Took one star off because the animatronic band glitched and would only play Candle In The Wind.
Manager Joe F.

Hi Eric, I'm so happy to hear our location brought you back to your childhood! Sorry about Chuck E.'s band glitching, but hey, who doesn't love Elton John!?!

★ ☆ ☆ ☆ ☆
Corson B.

HORRIBLE!! My family comes to this Chuck E. Cheese at least once a month, but after this last trip NEVER AGAIN. One, the racing game was impossible to win. Every time you passed through a tunnel, your car crashed. Even I, an adult, tried it and could not get through. Two, the prizes were total crap. My kids had over 500 tickets and all they got was a pamphlet about the dangers of landmines. Three, the movie that typically plays on the TVs *Chuck E. Cheese in the Galaxy 5000*, had been replaced by a graphic documentary about leprosy. Completely lost my appetite for my Pepperoni Bites. Giving this place one star because it smelled nice. Like rose and jasmine. But other than that, this place stinks!!
Manager Joe F.

Corson, from the bottom of my heart, I am so sorry about your negative experience at our Chuck E. Cheese. Please call me at 202-224-2541 and I can offer you a refund and discounts for future visits.

Corson B.

AS IF, I'd want to visit again. What are you doing to rectify this situation for other guests?

Manager Joe F.

Corson, I assure you my team and I are doing everything in our power to fix this. We have taken the racing game off the game floor, restored the prizes, and turned off the TVs. I have contacted the Church of England and fingers crossed the Archbishop of Canterbury gets back to me with further instructions.

★ ★ ★ ★ ★

Elisabeth D.

Don't know why all the negative reviews! I brought my grandkids here last weekend. They loved the games, and I had the loveliest conversation with a beautiful young woman. When she told me she was a grandma too, I could scarcely believe it! She didn't look a day over thirty. After she left, the manager came over with a free pizza "for my patience." Funny enough, the cheese was browned in a way that looked exactly like the face of the lovely young woman! LOL!

Manager Joe F.

Elisabeth, so happy you had a great time at Chuck E. Cheese. Did the young woman mention any unfinished business she needed help with or any reason she was at our Chuck E. Cheese? Please call me at 202-224-2541 and if you can offer any guidance, I'll give you free pizza for life.

★ ★ ☆ ☆ ☆

Travis S.

Came here for my nephew's soccer team fundraiser. I wanted to give this place more stars, but had a very disturbing encounter with my waitress Camilla. Ordered two pepperoni pizzas, cheesy bread, and sodas. Never received my food, but did receive quite the show. All the lights in the place went out except for the animatronic band. They stopped singing, and the chicken started talking in a British accent, saying she couldn't leave this Earthly plane until her royal duties were done. Camilla bursts out of the kitchen with a huge knife and hacks at the giant animatronic chicken. The chicken is writhing and screaming and Camilla is ripping this thing apart. All the kids are crying. Someone pulls a fire alarm and the sprinklers go off. Last thing I saw before I got out of there was Camilla screaming, "I'm sorry, I'm sorry, please go toward the light," at the dismembered body of the electric chicken. Giving it two stars, one for the light-up Skee-Ball game and one for the manager graciously giving $200 to my nephew's soccer team.

Manager Joe F.

Hi Travis, again, I cannot apologize enough for ruining your nephew's fundraiser. I hope the $200 (from my own wallet) is enough to get The Tornadoes new uniforms. I'd ask that if any members of the press call you for comment, you focus on the fun Skee-Ball and not all other aspects of your experience.

★ ☆ ☆ ☆ ☆
Jessica S.

Tried to bring my kids here last weekend, but it was empty. I guess it has closed.

Manager Joe F.

Hi Jessica, we aren't closed! Despite all the false rumors and that negative piece in The Guardian, we're open for fun! The Archbishop of Canterbury himself flew here to bless the building and help any lingering spirits cross over. We even got him to sign a photo to put on our Chuck E. Celeb Wall of Fame. But you won't hear that on CNN! Also, Camilla is doing fine. Chuck E. Cheese corporate paid for three counseling sessions for her and she's found a new job at Jo-Ann Fabric.

★ ★ ★ ★ ★
Matt R.

Had so much fun last year, we celebrated my son's ninth birthday here. Another stellar experience. Chuck E. Cheese even sang my son happy birthday as they brought out his cake! An FYI to management, the spirit of Napoleon Bonaparte is in your uni-sex bathroom.

Manager Joe F.

Thanks for the heads up! We've contacted the French consulate and recommend customers not use that bathroom unless they want to hear about choking of British trade routes while they pee.

Reasons For My Recent Weight Gain

Greetings Friends, Family, Acquaintances, Coworkers, and Complete Strangers,

I have gained weight! What does this mean for me? I had to buy a new pair of pants for work. What does this mean for you? You believe my health, safety, sanity, and future romantic prospects have been annihilated by a 15% increase in my body weight.

I know what's coming. You'll send me articles about how Weight Watchers is feminist now, or tell me being overweight is more dangerous than smoking meth, or scream "Fat Bitch" at me on the street.

For the sake of everyone's time, I'm sending out this handy list of rejoinders. Choose the retort that speaks to you and then take your questions, passive aggressive texts, or jeers and shove them up the bodily cavity of your choice.

Why have you gained weight?

Before I go camping, I want to make myself as big as possible, so I threaten predators.

I lost my winter coat, and this was cheaper than buying a new one.

I'm taking a new medication and the only way I can get the pills down my throat is by coating them with lard.

Four years ago, I bought a $200 Khaleesi Halloween costume and have felt obligated to wear it every year because of the expense. Now that it no longer fits, I don't have to carry an egg with me to parties every Halloween.

I saw one smiling fat woman in a bikini on Instagram.

I saw one chonky pupper on Twitter.

I saw one episode of Shrill.

I made a deal with Smucker's that if I eat an entire jar of Smucker's Goober Peanut Butter and Jelly with every meal for a year, they will put my face on the label.

Keep this a secret, but I've been chosen to colonize Mars and they need me to gain weight so I don't float away.

You caught me in the hyperphagia stage of my hibernation cycle.

My fetish is hearing people rave about Whole30.

I wanted to try a Tyra Banks style fat suit experiment, but I couldn't afford the fat suit.

In my youth, I fell in love with a large animal veterinarian, but we drifted apart. Now, in an attempt to reconnect, I am gaining so much weight my doctor has to take me to his office to use his industrial animal scale.

I got so hungry I ate my own thyroid.

Eight months ago I loaned my metabolism to a friend. We haven't spoken since, and it feels awkward to reach out just because I want something back.

Lizzo.

I've gotten an exciting opportunity for my ass to be filmed for stock footage of fat people for fear-mongering news reports.

I've gotten an exciting opportunity to travel the sideshow circuit as a Fat Lady, eating greased muffins as children pelt me with pennies.

I've gotten an exciting opportunity to work for NOAA's National Data Buoy Center as a weather buoy off the coast of North Carolina.

I'm trying to seduce the ghost of Peter Paul Rubens.

I'm part of a SAW-style torture game. I'm full of keys and the bigger I get, the harder it is for others to cut them out of me.

Like a Pokémon, this is the next phase of my evolution. I can also fart fire and speak only my own name.

I want to be buried in a piano case.

I want to make my body into a walking, talking reminder that gaining weight isn't inherently bad and perhaps the societal system you've bought in to for your entire life was only created to keep you focused on your waistline rather than issues of actual importance.

I want tig ol' bitties.

The Starlight Ball

Oh James, this is the best night of my life. Dancing with you at the Country Club's Starlight Ball. We're in the middle of the dancefloor, surrounded by couples, but when I'm in your arms, it feels as if we're the only two people on Earth.

What are you thinking about, darling? Yes, I agree, it is strange that just last week we were complete strangers, but then your stray frisbee landed near where I was sunning myself on the beach and now we're inseparable. But that's love, I guess.

What am I thinking about? Oh, it's silly. You wouldn't want- well, all right. Pressed so close, my head resting on your steady shoulder, I can't help thinking how easy it would be for me to bite off your ear.

I mean, it would be so simple. I could lean over just an inch, my warm breath tickling the side of your face. You think I'm going to whisper a sexy secret. About to tell you I want you to take my virginity on the cool Virginia sand as the waves crash onto the shore, echoing our moans of pleasure. But instead, I open my mouth, take your entire ear between my teeth, and bite down as hard as I can.

No, silly. It's a daffy idea. Don't you sometimes have thoughts that pop into your head as though God dropped them in there by accident?

Your whole ear comes off in one bite. Blood bursts from the side of your face, soaking my pink taffeta gown. You scream and fall to the ground. The band's last jarring note hangs sourly in the evening air. No one saw it happen. One moment everyone's swirling in time with the smooth jazz and the next they're confronted by a man clutching the side of his face, blood pooling on the black-and-white checkered dance floor. Everyone wonders what happened, but I just smile, your entire right ear tucked behind my teeth.

Of course, I wouldn't actually do it. It's a passing fancy. Like last week I was at Foster's Pharmacy, and I had the impulse to order a chocolate egg cream. I've never ordered one before. Never even thought about it. But there I was, on the verge of ordering this totally unknown drink. It's like that.

Everyone stands still for an infinite moment, before a girl's scream punctures the silence. Old Lou calls for an ambulance, but you're losing so much blood Ricky and the boys insist on driving you to the hospital themselves. As the men argue about the safest course of action, I bend down and stroke your bloody cheek. There's betrayal in your eyes, but we both know I don't deserve it. In our week of fun and sun and surf, I've never once promised not to wrap my crimson lips around your ear and bite. Perhaps that's love. Hoping so many unspoken tragedies never come to pass.

Of course, I won't bite off your ear, James. Just like I didn't order that chocolate egg cream. I stuck with the vanilla malt. Simply because I have a thought, doesn't mean I'll act on it. It's what separates us from the animals.

In the backseat of Ricky's car to the hospital, you lay your head in my lap. By this point, you're barely conscious. You lay facing my sequined bodice, the hole where your ear used to be pointing up, the raw flesh smarting in the cool evening air. At the hospital, the doctors ask what happened. I don't say a word. Everyone assumes I'm in shock, but it's really because I have your ear in my mouth.

James, you're hurting my wrist! You can't be angry at me for thinking. I know you think about other girls, but as long as you don't do anything, it's fine. As long as I don't actually rip your ear off like a rabid pit bull, then you can't get mad.

The doctors stop the bleeding. Everyone at the country club searches the dancefloor for your ear, but no one can find it. I slip out of the emergency room and take the stairs up to the roof of the hospital. My tongue slips back and forth between the slick salty meat of the back and the waxy skin of the front of your ear. It's so soft, I could swallow it without fear of choking. On the roof, I spit your ear into my hand.

What do I do with your ear? Wouldn't you like to know?

Maybe I'll drop it off the hospital roof and it will land in a woman's hat and she'll drive far away. Next Sunday she'll wear the hat to church. When she bends her head in prayer, your ear will fall out. Everyone will think it's a miracle.

Maybe I'll take it downstairs and hand it to a doctor and he'll sew it back onto your head. The procedure works because I kept the ear viable in my warm, moist mouth. And you'll have to marry me, because I've had a part of you inside me, not in the traditional way, but it counts all the same.

Maybe I'll hold on to your ear. I'll put it in my velvet clutch, the blood staining the silk lining. We're both changed, forever and always, because I took something from you. A souvenir of first love. Sometimes late at night you swear you can still hear my voice, softly whispering to you in the place your ear used to be.

But of course, I'd never do it. It was just a funny little thought. And I can tell you don't wash behind your ears.

RSVP Poems

Graham and Kristie
So lucky to be expecting a baby
Regretfully, I will not be attending your Prince or Princess
Gender Reveal
For Gender is a construct
The Binary is a prison of our own making
And in college, I fucked you both

Hey Ryan
I'm marking Interested on this Facebook invite
To your recorder recital
Even though I am not
At all
Interested

Laura
Regarding your Full Moon Ritual this Friday
With your Candles, Palo Santo, Crystals, Tarot Cards,
Pendulums, Feathers, Herbs, Pentagrams, Amulets,
Incense, Oils, Tree Bark, Dowsing Rods, and Bundles of Twigs
I'll be there
Not to set my intentions and cleanse my chakras
But
Because you borrowed my portable speaker
And I'd really like it back

Your boyfriend
Is doing improv
In a basement

Dear Seema
What makes you think
I will like him more
After seeing this

I apologize, Melanie
I must RSVP No to your wedding
For it is on a plantation
And you asked guests to dress in period-appropriate clothing
And while I am willing to rent a fluffy gown
My husband fears his tattered rags might stain
Your lovely white dress
And what a shame
That would be

Brunch
At nine am
On a Sunday
An hour away from my home
Save me a seat
Like Elijah
Maybe I'll make it this year

Tamyra
Your daughter is selling Girl Scout cookies
And it would mean so much
If I'd stop by the table set up outside of Kroger
And place my order
Now Tamyra,
I don't mean this as hyperbole
But I would venture though nine circles of Hell
For one box of Samoas
So tell your daughter when she sees me at her table
She can put me down

For twenty

Yes, Dahlia, I attended your baby's Baptism
But I will not attend yours
For you are old enough to know better

Dearest Tom
With a heavy heart
I must inform you I
will not
be attending your Dirty Thirty Karaoke Birthday
Because
You know why
Really
You're going to make me say it
Really, Tom
Ok
My roommate told me you sexually assaulted her
And unlike our other friends
I *Don't Stop Believin'*

The Mark Of The Devil

"Father Mulcahy?"

The Priest looked up from the game of minesweeper he was playing on his computer. He still had fifteen minutes before the 10:30 confession. His secretary, Missi, peered from the doorway. He wasn't a tyrant, but everyone knew 10-10:30 was minesweeper time.

"What is it, Missi?"

"Mr. and Mrs. Holzmann are here with their baby boy."

"Father Lewis is handling baptisms. Send them to him." He clicked on a gray square. "Oh Cheesewhiz, a mine."

"Father, it's not about a Baptism. It's a more sensitive matter. They know of your... reputation."

"Another one? That was an informational lecture on the history of exorcism in the Church. I am not Damien Karras!" Ever since he gave that silly talk last October, part of the Public Library's Halloween events, people had been popping out of the woodwork asking him to remove demons from friends, loved ones, and in one particularly annoying case, an entire family of opossums in a cardboard box.

"If you remember," said Missi, "Mr. Holzmann made a generous donation to restore the stained glass in the sanctuary."

Father Mulcahy sighed and waved for her to bring them in.

The sniffling Holzmanns shuffled into his office. Mr. Holzmann wore a slick suit, looking every inch a corporate bond trader. Mrs. Holzmann, normally dressed in a Nancy Reagan skirt set, instead wore a stained Simpsons sweatshirt and had the hair of a woman who slept in a wind tunnel. She clutched a mound of blankets to her chest.

"Thank you for seeing us Father," said Mr. Holzmann, "We had nowhere else to turn. The doctors weren't helpful. You would think at a Catholic hospital the doctors would take this kind of thing seriously."

"What type of thing are you referring to?" asked Father Mulcahy. He guessed it was a birthmark or extra-large mole. Something hypervigilant parents could mistake as a mark of the devil.

"It's awful," shrieked Mrs. Holzmann, her body shaking with sobs, "I can't believe this... this thing was inside me."

Father Mulcahy pulled back the blanket and looked at the baby in Mrs. Holzmann's arms. He screamed.

What do you think is wrong with the baby? Send your guess (in a paragraph, drawing, or poem) to 666evilbaby69@gmail.com.

The best guess will receive guaranteed admission to The Kingdom of Heaven.

And Now A Word From Our Sponsors

Penny Pinching Tips for the Morally Bankrupt is
brought to you by these fine businesses.

Sugar Sisters Bakery: Sweet treats for every occasion. Want a personalized message on your cake? We'll do that too as long as the message is "One hundred and nine people died on March 9, 1953, in the rush to view Josef Stalin's coffin." We're open to spelling "Josef" in a couple different ways, but beyond that, the message is non-negotiable.

Ardie Family Pharmacy: Pills as big as your head! Finish the El Grande Lipitor in thirty minutes or less and your prescription is free.

Pretty Paws Dog Grooming: We DO NOT groom babies. AGAIN, that's a big NO on cleaning dirty toddlers, putting them in the dog dryer, spraying them with perfume, and leaving them in a basket in the waiting room with a bow in their hair. NO NO NO! You should NEVER leave your baby unsupervised in our waiting room, ring a bell with the face of a dirty baby on it, then return two hours later to pick up your clean bundle of joy. ABSOLUTELY NOT. This is NOT a service we offer, and you should disregard all Yelp reviews to the contrary (no matter how complimentary of our skills in washing babies).

The Blue Orchid Bed and Breakfast: Haunted since '19.

The Blue Orchid Bed and Breakfast: Haunted since 2019.

The Blue Orchid Bed and Breakfast: A woman killed her husband and herself in our Violet Suite in September 2019. You're perfectly fine visiting spooky B&Bs where murders happened a hundred years ago. Just because the victim owned a MacBook

Pro, it's "tasteless" and "too soon" to advertise haunted tours.

Murphy's Pub and Grub: The slickest bathroom floors in Chicago!

Belia's Bridal Boutique: The only bridal boutique where we will talk you out of getting married. We have troubling statistics. We have testimonies from women saying their marriage was a mistake. We've hired a private investigator to follow your fiancé and write down all the problematic shit he says when you're not around. If you have cold feet, come to Belia's and we'll plunge them into the liquid nitrogen of truth. Belia's Bridal Boutique, we haven't sold a dress yet and God willing we never will!

The Magic Kingdom

"Honey, stay here," shouted Terrance's mom, "I'm going inside to look at Mrs. Melvin's Swarovski crystal lion cubs."

Terrance gave her a thumbs up and continued digging through the crate of vinyl records on Mrs. Melvin's driveway. All down the block were similar set-ups. People emptying out the crap in their houses so neighbors could take it to replace the crap they had sold at their garage sales. An ouroboros of Precious Moments figurines and casserole dishes.

Terrance didn't have a record player, but he thought if he bought some records it might plant the idea in his mom's head to buy him one. She hated purposeless things. Knick knacks, broken toys, unemployed Uncle Geoff. Without something to do, what excuse did something have for existing? He bet she was only going inside to look at those stupid glass lions to get out of the heat for ten minutes and score a La Croix from Mrs. Melvin's fridge.

His friend Neveah's older brother Kent had a record player and Kent was so cool his parents had bought him a motorcycle for his sixteenth birthday. It's like they knew they were raising a badass and didn't want to get in his way. Neveah said Kent was always inviting girls over to "listen to records." Terrance knew this was a euphemism for making out, but even having a girl sitting on his bed listening to the same sounds as him seemed mind-blowingly intimate.

In his head it was a straight line from records, to record player, to having girls over, to manhood. He was almost thirteen. It was time to grow up.

❖ ❖ ❖

"He's not okay, Frank. He hasn't gotten out of bed in a week. He won't eat. Won't bathe. I told him Walter had a job for him at the Tupperware factory and the boy growled at me. Like a wild animal."

"He'll be fine, Ellie. He's shell shocked. I bet you'd be growling too if you got your entire future snatched away by Charlie's stray bullet. That boy was going to be a Four-Star General, but now... Give him time."

"I have. He's been home from Vietnam for-"

Lee put his pillow over his head, trying to block out his parents' concerned conversation drifting up from the living room. His pillow smelled terrible after a week of hosting his filthy head, but it was better than listening to his father lament his son's lost potential. A future strewn with medals and epaulets, reduced to pushing a button on a machine in a factory ten hours a day for the next forty years. He pressed his face deeper into his musky pillow and cried.

Foreigner, Eddie Money, ZZ Top, The Alan Parsons Project. This was grandpa music. His mom would never believe Terrance needed a record player to listen to Shirley Caesar Sings Her Gospel Favorites.

Terrance scanned the tables of baby clothes, board games, and half-burned candles for anything else he might use to spruce up his boring bedroom. In the movies, teen boys always had bedrooms that reflected their "teen-ness." Sports trophies, bikini posters, crossed hockey sticks hanging above their beds. His mom would rather he hung a dead opossum on his wall than a sexy poster, but maybe he could find a motorcycle calendar or a sports jersey as a physical manifestation of his maturity.

Nothing on the Melvin's cracked driveway fulfilled his masculine requirements. The closest thing was a set of golf clubs, but they were more "middle aged business dad" than "cool teen with lots of friends." Anyway, the closest Terrance would ever be to a golfer was playing mini golf in Tampa with his cousins. And even then, he'd cried when he lost his ball in the platypus pond.

Disappointed that his personal mission had failed, he looked for items his mom might enjoy. A cake pan in the shape of a butterfly? A bag of shells from Sanibel Island? Both things she might appreciate, but neither worth their $5 green stickers. He squeezed past a woman digging through cloth diapers and snagged a quart mason jar. Last week Terrance had broken one of his mom's jars by filling it with marbles to make it into a musical instrument. This would serve as a gift and an apology. It had no price, but he was confident the spare change in his BB-8 wallet would cover it.

Lee's father had carried the TV set up to Lee's room and put it on a table right next to his bed so he could reach the knobs without getting up. His mom never let him watch TV much growing up, saying it would rot his brain. Lee pressed the on button, hoping the grainy images would turn his mind into soup. For thirty minutes he watched Monty Hall make deals with screaming people in wacky costumes. He felt a perverse joy watching contestants' faces fall when they traded their Amana microwave ovens for Zonks.

Commercials were less satisfying. No one was ever sad in commercials. Or if they were unhappy, it was only for a few seconds until a new brand of laundry detergent solved all life's problems. On the screen he saw a blonde girl in a white night-gown running around the forest. As she ran, she met grotesque cartoon figures. Over and over she asked if they knew the way to The Magic Kingdom. Finally, she awakened from her nightmare and opened her curtains, the sun on her tiny face, and smiling at a giant fairy-tale castle. And she'd be flying to Walt Disney World on Eastern Airlines.

Huh, he remembered hearing about Disney World from his buddy Sam, who had worked construction for the park the summer before their senior year of high school. Lee had taken a job flipping burgers at McDonald's, in his mind a much more grown-up job than building Cinderella's castle. But Lee had tried on manhood and it was not so comfortable. Perhaps what he needed was to take a ride in a spinning teacup.

◆ ◆ ◆

"How much?" Terrance asked the dozing old couple sitting behind the payment table. The women had tightly permed gray hair, and both wore World's Best Grandma t-shirts. They must have been sharing the title.

"What do you think, Myra? How much for the jar?" asked the one on the left.

"Is there a tag on it, Ora? My daughter warned me about giving deals to handsome men." She gave him an exaggerated wink and even though the flirting was from an old lesbian grandma, Terrance felt a blush creep up his neck.

"I wouldn't want to take advantage of you, young ladies," said Terrance, deepening his voice. He'd heard his dad call the mean old woman at the bank 'young lady' and she'd been so pleased she'd let Terrance have a whole handful of hard candy from her bowl. Flirting was lying you didn't get in trouble for.

"Young ladies!" said Ora. Both giggled at the lanky tween. "Well sir, the jar itself is worth ten cents, but it's what's inside that's really valuable."

Terrance examined the empty jar. He was about to unscrew the lid, when Myra said, "No, you'll let him out!"

"What? Is there a bug in here?" Terrance tapped the jar, hoping to wake up whatever the women were talking about.

"No, not a bug," said Ora, grinning so big he could see the edges of her dentures, "there's a ghost in that jar."

No glance passed between the women, a telltale sign that adults were pulling his leg. Terrance turned the jar in his hands, examining it from all angles. He didn't have a firm stance on whether ghosts existed. In the daylight hours, he didn't believe in any monsters, but at night a strange noise could convince him a demon from the depths of Hell was waiting under his bed to devour him whole.

"How do you know there's a ghost in here?" he asked.

"Because I put him in there," said Ora, "He was in the attic banging around all night. No one in the house could get any sleep. So I put on my crucifix, burned a bundle of sage, and trapped him in that very jar."

From the half an episode of a ghost hunting show he'd seen, this checked out. It would be pretty manly to have a whole ghost in his room. Last summer he had lightning bugs in a jar, this summer, a spirit doomed to walk the Earth forever. It wasn't a motorcycle, but it was badass, nonetheless.

Lee didn't dare tell his parents why his mood had changed. That he was drinking his milk and doing his stretches, so he was fit enough to walk around a theme park with Tinkerbell. But they were so pleased to see a sign of life in the smelly lump that had been laying in their son's bed, his parents didn't push for a reason.

"Lee, don't strain yourself," said his mother as he hobbled across the backyard.

"Let him go, he's almost made it all the way five times," said his father. His parents sat in lawn chairs in the backyard. This evening's entertainment was their crippled son dragging his crap leg around in the Florida heat.

"I'm so proud of him," whispered his mother, leaning on his father's hairy arm.

Why did parents lower their voices for praise, but raise them in anger? Growing up his mother had no problem hollering at him for leaving dirty socks under his bed, but when he told her he'd earned an A in Mr. Linus's impossibly difficult physics class, she'd nodded and asked if he wanted corn with dinner.

"Me too. What a great boy we've got," whispered his father as Lee took a last shuddering step, then collapsed into a lawn chair.

Lee closed his eyes and tried to remember the last time his parents had been this proud of him. It had been the morning of his eighteenth birthday. His mom made pancakes with sprinkles mixed into the batter, and his father drove him straight to the recruitment office.

Four months later, after Basic and bureaucratic delays, he found himself on a plane headed to Vietnam. And for an entire year he'd followed orders to burn and shoot and kill and maim and do whatever it took to secure American victory. Until he'd caught a bullet in the knee. Then the talk of every soldier being necessary to the mission evaporated. The Army didn't need a soldier who couldn't walk more than a few steps without collapsing when they had plenty of fresh young bodies to throw into the line of fire.

The most vivid feeling from Lee's year on the front line wasn't fear, or anger, or regret, but embarrassment. Embarrassment that he'd signed up for this dirty, violent, despicable job based on propaganda. Movies featuring heroic soldiers fighting for their girl back home, posters showing the American flag being burned by the foul hand of Communism, and stories of his Grandpa who'd killed dozens of Nazis before they captured him and had shot himself in the head rather than risk giving up one American secret. And yes, he realized the irony of committing himself to this new propaganda about the happiest place on Earth peddled by a cartoon mouse. But if Lee was going to believe in something, he'd rather believe in something that didn't order him to set fire to civilian homes and shoot anyone who tried to escape.

Yes, he'd rather pledge his allegiance to Peter Pan.

"How much?" Terrance hoped the ghost in a jar was cheap enough he wouldn't have to ask his mom. She'd never give him money to buy a ghost. Not when it could be spent on practical things like new school shoes or replacing his lost retainer.

"Hmm, what do you think?" the women said to each other in unison. They both laughed, Ora holding onto Myra's sun hat as it flew off her head.

"You'd be doing us a favor taking it off our hands," said Myra.

"If you take him, you must swear cross your heart and hope to die to never open the jar. I bet he's not too happy being trapped in there," said Ora.

"I promise. I'll even put glue around the lid. My mom has a hot glue gun I can use." This was half a lie. His mom had a hot glue gun, but Terrance was not allowed to touch it.

"Okay, you can have it for one dollar, but no returns." Ora kept on with the disclaimers, but Terrance was already digging in his wallet for a crumpled dollar bill.

"Thank you for your business," said Myra, putting the dollar in the cash box.

The jar immediately felt heavier. And was that a swirl of smoke leaking from the rim? Terrance tightened the lid as hard as he could, keeping his hand on top for good measure. He could feel the lid pulsing under his palm, the ghost trying to get out.

"Terrance, what did you buy?" his mom asked, emerging from the Melvin's house carrying a cold Dr. Pepper.

"Not what, but who. Terrance will bring a new soul home with him today," said Ora. Terrance was even more confident the ghost was real. Adults might try to trick kids with spooky stories, but they wouldn't lie to other adults.

"An imaginary friend. Cute," said his mom.

"Yeah, imaginary," Terrance scoffed. He winked at the grandmas then turned to follow his mom who was making her way across the yard to the next neighbor's sale.

◆ ◆ ◆

Lee counted ceiling tiles as he sat in the dentist's office waiting room. His mother had dropped him off after noticing he only chewed on the right side of his mouth. A left molar had cracked in the haze of pain that was his last year. He barely noticed it anymore, his mouth adjusting to chew around it, but Lee had agreed with his mother he needed to get it fixed. He told himself that if he didn't have his teeth fixed, then he wouldn't be able to enjoy all the treats he'd eat at Disney World.

His trip to Disney World provided most of the motivation for Lee's actions. He needed to strengthen his leg so he could walk around the park. He needed to find a job so he could afford a ticket and maybe a souvenir. He needed to keep himself on a schedule so his mind didn't slip into the dark place, and he didn't blow his brains out before he could go.

The woman sitting next to him fanned herself with a magazine while her sons played with blocks at her feet. She swatted the larger one with the magazine when he hit his brother with a block.

"That's enough, Martin. You're almost nine years old. Stop acting like a child." The hygienist called for Simpson and the two boys disappeared with her. The moment they were gone, the woman kicked off her shoes and lit a cigarette. "Ungrateful little shits. We spent half their daddy's paycheck taking them to Disney World last weekend and all they do is complain they didn't get a picture with Daffy Duck."

"But he's a Looney Tune," said Lee.

"Exactly, but you try explaining copyright law to a couple of sugared up crotch goblins." She took a long drag of her cigarette, then blew out the smoke in an upward plume.

"How much were tickets to Disney World?" he asked. It was fate, sitting next to a woman with firsthand knowledge of the park.

"Oh, three or four bucks a person. Why? You got kids?"

"No."

The woman stared at him, waiting for an explanation. Lee was not about to explain himself to a complete stranger.

"My sister has a little girl. Thought I'd try to be World's Best Uncle and take her sometime."

"Oh good, for a minute I was worried you were a pervert."

Rage constricted his lungs and he bit down hard on his cracked molar, trying to focus on the pain. "I don't think a man who wants to go to Disney World is necessarily a pervert."

"Ha, he'd have to be pretty messed up in the head to think taking a ride on It's A Small World is better than-"

Bang.

The door to the dentist's office slammed and Lee was back there. A bullet ripped through his knee as he tripped on underbrush. He needed to go. Run. Hide. Get out of the line of fire. Why were the people around him just sitting there? Lee sprinted into the hot afternoon sun. Out of his left eye he saw the quiet street in front of him. Out of his right eye he saw a dense jungle. Lee wasn't sure which one was real. Was he back home or had he never left?

"Sir, sir," yelled a voice behind him.

Lee sprinted forward, so blinded by fear he never saw the car coming.

At home, Terrance put the jar on his bookshelf, wedged between Dune and The Fellowship of the Ring in case the ghost tried to tip the jar over and escape. Over the next few days Terrance didn't notice any side effects from bringing a ghost into the house. No flickering lights, no slamming cabinets, or mysterious footsteps. His mom even agreed to let him go to his classmate Zaina's co-ed thirteenth birthday party at her parent's beach house, so perhaps the ghost was good luck.

That is, until his younger cousins from Tampa decided

Zaina's birthday weekend would be the perfect time to visit. And now, instead of playing spin the bottle in Zaina's rec room, he would be dragged around The Magic Kingdom. He pleaded with his mom, telling her Disney was for babies, not young men who could practically almost basically kind of grow a mustache.

"It'll be fun, Terrance," said his mom as she chopped scallions to add to the soup simmering on the stove, "You have the rest of your life to be an adult."

"But my cousins are babies. Arthur still sucks his thumb."

"Bring along your imaginary friend. He can keep you company."

"He's not... ugh, whatever." Terrance ran upstairs and jammed the jar into his backpack before climbing into the backseat of his Uncle Geoff's minivan. Maybe he could scare his cousins by telling them he had a ghost in his bag? That could be fun.

In the security line, Terrance had to hand over his backpack for inspection. The sweaty woman wearing neon Mickey ears poked around in his backpack and pulled out the jar.

"Glass containers are prohibited on Disney property," she said, pointing to a sign listing banned items. She began to twist open the lid, when Terrance lunged forward.

"No, you'll let him escape!"

Startled by Terrance's yelling, the woman dropped the jar. It shattered on the concrete. The woman said something into a walkie talkie as Terrance tried to put the shards of the jar back together. Uncle Geoff came over and put a hand on Terrance's shoulder.

"What happened?"

Terrance stood up, trying not to cry. "It was... It had a..."

"It's okay, my boy. Let's get in there and I'll buy you a Dole Whip. How does that sound?"

Uncle Geoff took Terrance's hand and led him into the park, all three men entering The Magic Kingdom.

Acknowledgements

I started this project to stave off pandemic-related depression because I couldn't perform anymore. It (along with Lexapro) kind of worked. Wow, maybe God was right about depression. And it wouldn't have happened without these lovely people.

My best friend, Elisabeth del Toro. She read this whole book twice, has directed me, performed with me, listened patiently every time I pitched a sketch where a character bled from an unexpected orifice, and still wants to be friends with me. My editor, Nicole Cunningham. She was the first person to take the nonsense that leaked out of my fingers seriously. My brother, Charlie. I'm still waiting on the Foreword you threatened to write.

Thank you to every editor who has published my work online: Carrie Wittmer, Fiona Taylor, Brooke Preston, Caitlin Kunkel, Patty Terhune, Lillian Stone, Scarlet Meyer, Terry Heyman, Briana Haynie, Harmony Cox, Jonterri Gadson, Ginny Hogan, Mary Cella, Court Sullivan, James Folta, Marty Dundics, Alex Baia, Sarah James, Sarah Pappalardo, and Dima Kronfeld.
You read my words and agreed to put them on the internet. Are you ok?

Thank you to all of the members of these improv/sketch teams: On A Stick, Talking Birds, Potato Town, Mystery Bucket, Velvet Maserati, Post Mortem, Battle Axe, True Crimes, Betsy, Trigger Happy Jr., and Ride Or Die.
Thanks for being my friends, my teammates, and supporting

every scene I started by talking about death.

And to my parents. I wouldn't exist without you.

About The Author

Libby Marshall is a writer, performer, and tall person who lives in Chicago, IL. She graduated from The University of Illinois with a degree in Creative Writing and Political Science. Her writing has appeared on Reductress, Slackjaw, Points In Case, The Belladonna, The Offing, Little Old Lady, and The Weekly Humorist. She has written and performed two solo shows, many sketch shows, and more improv shows than is healthy. She loves candles that smell like desserts, funny podcasts, and scarves that are big enough to double as blankets.
See more of her work at: Libby-Marshall.com

Well, Well, Well

Look who's here.

You, dear reader have gotten the the very end of the book. Like me with a bag of dill pickle potato chips, you've turned this book upside down, hoping to get one more delicious crumb onto your hungry little tongue. You're in luck. Here are some jokes that found no home between these pages, but I couldn't stand to let die.

A husband puts on a clean shirt. It smells terrible, even though his wife just washed it. He asks her why his shirt smells bad.

"Oh, I must have mixed up the bleach and the milk again," says the wife.

"That explains it."

"Why the shirt smells bad?"

"No, why the kids were vomiting blood after breakfast."

A pregnant woman goes to a doctor seeking an abortion.

The doctor says, "Yes I'll give you the abortion, but you have to have sex with me afterward."

The woman asks if they can have sex before the abortion.

The doctor says, "No, how else would I stay in business?"

On the first day of class, an Atheist philosophy professor said that he would give any student an automatic A if they could prove God exists. This was a liberal East Coast college, so most of the students simply chuckled. Even the few Christian students knew better than to argue with this Atheist, for he made this offer at the beginning of every semester and had not been convinced in twenty years.

In the front row sat an ex-Navy Seal who loved Christ. He stood up and looked the professor straight in the eye.

"So, you think you can convince me God exists?" mocked the Atheist professor, "Be warned, I once debated a priest and made him commit suicide."

"I believe that Jesus Christ is my lord and savior," said the Navy Seal, "but I am not going to convince you that God exists."

"Why not?" challenged the professor with a grin like the ACLU.

"Because I just realized I'm in the wrong class. I thought this was The Nineteenth Century Novel with Professor Murison."

"That's across the hall in 217," said the Atheist Professor.

"Thanks," said the Navy Seal with the strength of an eagle, "Sorry for interrupting."

"No problem. Tell Professor Murison I say hi."

What's the best way to dress a dead baby?
Ranch

CPSIA information can be obtained
at www.ICGtesting.com
Printed in the USA
LVHW082200121122
733018LV00011B/689